CHIEF IN TECH

HOW **WOMEN** ARE **BREAKING**
THE **SILICON CEILING** AND
LEADING WITH IMPACT

CHIEF
IN

Global
Leaders
Guide

TECH

ANNA RADULOVSKI

Global CEO & Founder of WomenTech Network,
Chief in Tech Summit & Executive Women in Tech

WILEY

Published by John Wiley & Sons, Inc., Hoboken, New Jersey.
Published simultaneously in Canada.

For general information on our other products and services or for technical support, please contact our Customer Care Department within the United States at (800) 762-2974, outside the United States at (317) 572-3993 or fax (317) 572-4002.

Wiley also publishes its books in a variety of electronic formats. Some content that appears in print may not be available in electronic formats. For more information about Wiley products, visit our website at www.wiley.com.

Library of Congress Cataloging-in-Publication Data is Available:

ISBN: 9781394292660 (Cloth)
ISBN: 9781394292677 (ePub)
ISBN: 9781394292684 (ePDF)

Cover Design: Wiley
Author Photo: © WomenTech Network

SKY10100159_031825

Contents

Preface

Close your eyes for a minute and imagine the most prominent tech executives today. Who comes to mind? Is it the typical suspects—men whose names are now associated with innovation? Elon. Jeff. Mark. Yes, they established empires, but the real question is: Why not you?

You've seen the headlines. AI is transforming industries, robots are performing surgeries, self-driving cars are navigating our busy city streets. Technology is moving at a pace we've never seen before but isn't it ironic that leadership often stays stuck in the past? Despite all this innovation, only a small fraction of leaders are women. I've seen the glaring disparities firsthand—at conferences, in boardrooms, engineering teams, on panels, promotion rounds, and the list goes on.

But here's the thing—you belong in that space. You should be one of the leaders shaping the future of AI, robotics, and beyond. Too often, the decision-makers in tech don't reflect the rich diversity of the world they're transforming. And that needs to change. The tech industry needs you—your perspective, your creativity, and your leadership. We need diverse voices driving innovation that actually reflect the world we live in.

Maybe you've felt that nagging doubt when you're the only woman in the room, the frustration when your ideas are overlooked, or the exhaustion of having to prove yourself over and over again. Maybe you recall that moment when you're in a meeting, and your suggestion is met with silence, only to be echoed by someone else (ahem) and suddenly, it's genius. Or perhaps you've hesitated to speak up in meetings, worried you'll be labeled too aggressive or not assertive enough. Or maybe you're juggling the demands of career and personal life, wondering if it's possible to have both without compromising either.

These frustrations aren't just yours—they're shared by countless women in the tech industry. The fear of not being taken seriously, the isolation of being one of the few, the uncertainty of how to navigate a male-dominated industry. These feelings are real, and they can definitely hold us back. But you're not alone, and it doesn't have to be this way.

The mission of *Chief in Tech* is to help you transform frustrations into fuel, fears into courage, and aspirations into reality. Whether you're just starting your journey in tech, climbing the ladder, or already in a leadership position, this book is your guide to achieving success and making an impact. Packed with practical strategies, stories, and actionable steps, we'll explore how to take control of your career, overcome barriers, and thrive in leadership—no matter where you are in your journey. We'll dive into navigating biases, negotiating for your worth, establishing a personal brand, creating supportive networks, mastering leadership skills, and becoming a leader who succeeds while helping others rise with you.

Along the way, I'll share my own stories and those of incredible women who've faced similar challenges, emerged as leaders, and left their mark. We'll explore how you can leverage your unique strengths, amplify your voice, and reach new heights.

Now, you might be wondering, "Who am I to be writing this book? Why should you care about my story, my insights, or my experiences?" I get it. There are a lot of thought leaders out there talking about leadership, women in tech, and breaking barriers, so let me tell you why I'm here.

I've been in the thick of it. As the founder of the WomenTech Network, I've worked with thousands of women, tech leaders, and allies. We've built a global movement with more than 150,000 members pushing for change in an industry that desperately needs it. I've sat at the table with executives from some of the world's biggest companies—Amazon, Google, Meta, Microsoft, and JPMorgan Chase, to name a few. I've seen firsthand the challenges women face at every level, from entry-level to mid-level to the C-suite. And through it all, I've been on a mission: to break down the barriers that keep women from thriving in tech and to help us grow and succeed.

My journey wasn't straightforward. Like many of you, I've questioned my place in this space. I've battled imposter syndrome, navigated an industry that didn't always feel welcoming, and had to build my network and the community piece by piece. I know what it's like to be the only woman in the room, to have your ideas dismissed, or to feel like you have to work twice as hard just to be noticed.

And that's why I'm so passionate about this book—because I know I'm not the only one who has felt this way. I've spoken with countless women who've had similar experiences, and I know that together, we can change the narrative.

Chief in Tech isn't simply my journey—it's our journey. It reflects the collective experiences of women who've navigated this male-dominated field and still found a way to thrive. Through the wisdom of those who have already blazed a trail, we work to open doors for the next generation. Together, we are building a future where women in tech are no longer the exception, but the norm.

Ultimately, *Chief in Tech* focuses on rewriting the rules. It aims to ensure the tech industry includes different perspectives, welcomes talent from all backgrounds, and truly represents the people shaping the future. It drives meaningful change at every level, creating spaces where women are seen, heard, valued, recognized, and celebrated—and where we don't just participate but lead with impact.

The more I thought about it, the more determined I became to take action. That's why I wrote *Chief in Tech*. This book doesn't just recognize the challenge; it's about stepping up and leading the change.

Let's not wait for permission. The tech revolution is already here—and it's time for us to lead it.

1

Overcoming Bias, Systemic Challenges, and Imposter Syndrome

Women belong in all places where decisions are being made.
It shouldn't be that women are the exception.
—Ruth Bader Ginsburg, former Associate Justice of the
Supreme Court of the United States

Imagine this: You've been working tirelessly, putting in extra hours, tackling complex projects, and contributing significantly to your team's success. The annual review is just around the corner, and you're feeling optimistic that your efforts will be recognized. You've put in the work, delivered results, and even exceeded your targets. Promotion, here we come!

But then, the performance review happens. Your manager acknowledges your hard work but starts talking about "areas for growth" and suggests revisiting the promotion next year. Meanwhile, your male colleague—who you've been helping throughout the year—gets the promotion instead. Frustrating? Absolutely. Surprising? Unfortunately, not so much.

If this scenario hits close to home, trust me, you're not alone. I can't count how many times I've heard this same story from women across all levels in tech. Whether they're new to the workforce, stuck in mid-career limbo, pushing toward the C-suite, or competing for a seat on the board, the barriers are always there, lurking. It often feels like you're running a race where the finish line keeps shifting just as you're about to cross it—working twice as hard for half the recognition.

So, why does this keep happening? In an industry that's all about innovation and disrupting the status quo, why are we still wrestling with outdated biases and systemic challenges?[1]

Let's dive into this together, since understanding the problem is the first step toward changing it.

The Gender Leadership Gap and Common Barriers Women Face in the Workplace

The gender leadership gap isn't just a matter of numbers (sure, numbers don't lie); it's a reflection of deep-rooted systemic biases and historical barriers that have been in place for, well frankly, way too long. For all the progress we've made, women in tech still make up less than one fifth of leadership roles, despite entering the workforce in equal numbers to men.

- **C-suite Representation**: Women hold only 12.4% of C-suite positions in STEM according to the World Economic Forum.[2]

- **Senior Executive Roles in AI**: Women hold less than 14% of senior executive positions, according to a global analysis of 1.6 million AI professionals.[3]

- **Chief Technology Officer Positions**: Women hold only 20.2% of Chief Technology Officer positions in mid-market tech firms according to Grant Thornton.[4]

And it gets much worse for women of color, Latina women, and other minorities. Only 3% of computing roles are held by African-American women, and 2% by Hispanic American/Latina women.[5]

But why does the leadership gap persist?

It starts with gender stereotyping. From an early age, many girls are subtly nudged away from leadership[6] or technical roles. Society often paints tech as a "guy thing," steering girls toward fields perceived as more "suitable."[7]

Even a simple visit to a toy store shows a clear picture: The aisles are divided—one side brimming with pink, sparkles, and "cute" items, while the other is a world of action, adventure, and building sets. Girls' toys encourage caregiving, like dolls and tea sets, while boys' toys emphasize boldness and construction—science kits, action figures, and Lego. The unspoken message is clear: girls are meant to care and look pretty, while boys are meant to build and conquer.

While boys are encouraged to be bold adventurers, girls are often steered toward being polite, thoughtful, and "nice."[8] Don't get me wrong, nurturing is great, but it shouldn't limit us from pursuing leadership. In fact, a KPMG study[9] found that only 34% of women were encouraged to "share their point of view" while growing up. This early conditioning doesn't just vanish when we step into the workplace. It lingers, influencing how we see ourselves and, unfortunately, how others see us too.

Radhika Krishnan, General Manager, Amazon Web Services (AWS)[10] shared that "the higher up you go, women executives tend to become a minority." She explained that "as humans, we unintentionally stereotype"— with a common mental model of a successful C-suite executive as typically a white male. For Krishnan, the path forward means "putting the spotlight on people who don't fit the mold" and reshaping these perceptions to create a more inclusive vision of who can lead.

I've had countless conversations with successful women who had to unlearn these internalized norms. They had to give themselves permission to take up space, to voice their ideas confidently, and to lead without constantly second-guessing themselves.

It continues with the "broken rung."[11] It's that first critical step up to management where women often get stuck. For every 100 men promoted to a managerial position, only about 86 women make the same leap,[12] and the numbers are even lower for women of color. It's like starting a marathon with your shoelaces tied together—hardly a fair race.

It's an early disadvantage that ripples through our entire careers. No wonder that by the time we reach mid-career, the gap between male and female leaders becomes a chasm.

This isn't because women lack ambition or skills. Studies[13] show that women are just as likely as men to aspire to leadership roles. The difference is, men are more likely to get tapped on the shoulder for those opportunities.

And then there's the likability penalty[14]—one of the most insidious barriers. Ever noticed how a man can be assertive and is seen as a strong leader, but a woman doing the same is labeled as aggressive or unapproachable?

Women in leadership often feel forced to choose between being likable or being seen as competent. If women are assertive, they're often perceived as less likable compared to men who act the same way. If women are warm and approachable, some might think they lack leadership strength. This is what's called the "Double Bind Dilemma."[15] It's like women have to constantly be balancing on a tightrope, trying to be both likable and competent, while men don't have to deal with this.

All of this builds up to the glass ceiling[16]—or in the tech world, the silicon ceiling—that barrier we bump up against when climbing the corporate ladder. And even if you manage to break through, you might find yourself on the glass cliff,[17] stepping into leadership roles only when the company is already in crisis, practically setting you up for failure from the start. Women are often given these high-risk positions as a way to signal "diversity" or "progress." If things go south, it's easier to pin the blame on the "failed female leader."[18]

Take Marissa Mayer's tenure at Yahoo as an example.[19] She stepped into a CEO role when the company was already in decline, fighting an uphill battle from day one. It's not that women can't handle tough roles—far from it—but it's telling that we often get the call when the ship is already sinking.

The fact is, the tech world still clings to outdated notions of what leadership looks like,[20] which often favors traits like assertiveness, dominance, and competitiveness—qualities traditionally associated with men.

But here's the thing—it doesn't have to be this way. We're going to explore how you can navigate these challenges, and yes, we'll dive into practical steps you can take to break through these barriers. It's not going to be a walk in the park, but together, we can change the narrative one woman at a time.

So, why are these barriers so stubborn, especially in an industry that prides itself on innovation? It's because these obstacles aren't just external—they're woven into the very fabric of workplace culture.

One of the biggest culprits is systemic bias. You may have found yourself in a room full of decision-makers who don't look like you, don't share your background, and might even question whether you belong there. For many women, that's the reality. Biases—often unconscious—lead to assumptions about what leaders look like,[21] and surprise, surprise, it's usually not us. When companies picture their next CTO or VP, they're often envisioning someone who fits the mold: male, typically white, and often groomed through "traditional" leadership paths that have historically excluded women and minorities.

This bias shows up in performance reviews,[22] in the opportunities handed out, and in the expectations placed on women versus men. Women are often judged on their past performance, while men are judged on their leadership potential.[23] This plays a huge role in why fewer women are promoted early in their careers, which means fewer women get the chance to gain leadership experience, leading to fewer women in the C-suite and on boards.

Neveen Awad, Managing Director and Partner at The Boston Consulting Group,[24] nailed it when she said, "Promoting women early and often is critical. Those first promotions set a precedent—they build confidence, help women see themselves as leaders, and most importantly, show everyone else that women belong in these roles."

For every Sheryl Sandberg or Ginni Rometty, there are countless women who've been passed over—not because they lacked the skills or ambition, but because the system wasn't designed for them to succeed.

There's the infamous workplace environment, especially in tech, where the "bro culture" can sometimes feel like an impenetrable fortress. Maybe it's the after-work drinks you're not invited to, the inside jokes you don't find funny (or appropriate), or the networking events—over beer, at the golf course, or during weekend getaways? They seem tailor-made for anyone but women. These exclusions might seem minor individually, but together they build a wall that can be tough to climb.

This culture shows up in meetings, in decision-making processes, and in who gets a seat at the table—both literally and figuratively. Being left out of informal networks means missing out on crucial conversations where decisions are often made long before any official meeting happens.

And when we do make it into these spaces, we're sometimes met with microaggressions—those subtle, often unintentional slights that undermine our competence and chip away at our confidence. Comments like, "You're pretty technical for a woman," "Who's helping you with your kids while you're working?" or "You don't look like a CTO." They might just seem harmless on the surface, but over time, they start to sting. They're like tiny paper cuts; one might not slow you down, but a hundred of them can be debilitating.

Think about moments when you've been interrupted in meetings, when your emails are met with skepticism, or when you're left off important threads. Or when you're asked to take notes in a meeting where you're actually the most senior person in the room. It's these everyday moments that reinforce the message: "You don't quite belong here."

Microaggressions are those small but persistent, everyday comments or behaviors that, over time, start to erode a person's confidence and sense of belonging. They might seem insignificant in the moment, but their cumulative effect is powerful—not just for individuals but for teams. As Lori Nishiura Mackenzie, Co-founder at Stanford VMware Women's Leadership Innovation Lab,[25] notes, "One issue with microaggressions is that we often overlook their impact on the team, viewing them as only affecting the individual. Microaggressions hurt the team's overall performance."

Elaine Montilla, CTO at Pearson,[26] shared how she faced microaggressions throughout her career. From being talked over in meetings to seeing her ideas credited to others, she had to learn to assert herself. Studies show that women are interrupted 2.5 times more often than men in meetings.[27] Montilla reflected on how she developed the confidence to respond in those moments, saying it's crucial to find a way to reclaim your voice, even when it feels like climbing Everest amidst daily slights.

I remember a powerful moment with Kamala Harris during the 2020 Vice Presidential debate when, after being interrupted by then-Vice President Mike Pence, she firmly responded, "I'm speaking."[28] The moral of the story: your point, idea or feedback has value, so finish your thought, you are speaking! (See Table 1.1.)

In the moment, it's normal to feel frustrated or even angry when dealing with microaggressions. But addressing them—calmly and assertively—not only lets you advocate for yourself but also contributes to a more inclusive workplace culture. And no, microaggressions aren't minor annoyances; they reflect deeper systemic issues within workplace cultures that were never designed with women in mind.

Table 1.1   Microaggressions, Scenario, and How to Respond

Microaggression	Scenario	How to Respond
Interruptions	You're presenting a point in a meeting, and someone cuts you off before you finish.	Calmly say, "Please hold your thought for a moment, I'd like to finish my point," or "I appreciate your input, but I'd like to finish my point first" and continue speaking.
Credit Theft	You suggest a strategy that's ignored until someone else rephrases it and gets the credit.	Politely interject with, "I'm glad you agree with the strategy I mentioned earlier," to reclaim ownership of your idea. Allies can support you with, "As [Your Name] mentioned earlier…"
Assumptions of Inferiority	A colleague says, "You're very technical for a woman."	Respond with confidence, "I've been working in tech for 15 years; technical expertise is a core part of my career."
Exclusion from Informal Networks	Important discussions happen during informal gatherings you're not invited to.	Proactively suggest inclusive team activities or directly express your interest: "I'd love to join the next planning session. Can you keep me in the loop?"

(continued)

Table 1.1   (*Continued*)

Microaggression	Scenario	How to Respond
Mansplaining	Someone explains something to you in a condescending way, assuming you lack knowledge on the subject.	Gently interrupt with, "Thanks, I'm familiar with this topic. Let's dive into the specifics."
Tone Policing	You're discussing an issue, and someone responds, "Calm down, you're overreacting."	Say, "I'm emphasizing this because it's important. Let's focus on the points I'm raising please."

Look, I know this all might seem a bit daunting. But the first step in tackling these challenges is acknowledging them. By understanding the barriers—whether they're stereotypes, cultural norms, or systemic biases—we can start to navigate around them, over them, or, when necessary, bulldoze right through them.

And remember, you don't have to do it alone. Building a strong network, finding mentors and allies, and supporting others can create a ripple effect that leads to broader change (more on that in Chapter 5).

Every time one of us speaks up, challenges a bias, or supports another woman, we're not just helping ourselves—we're paving the way for those who come after us.

So let's keep the conversation going. Let's share our stories, our strategies, and yes, even our frustrations. Because together, we can create a workplace culture that's not just tolerable, but truly empowering for everyone.

Imposter Syndrome: The Battle Within

You know that nagging voice inside your head that whispers, "You're not good enough"? That's imposter syndrome talking. Almost every woman I know in tech has felt it at some point, no matter how successful she is.

Research confirms this with 75% of female executives experiencing Imposter Syndrome.[29] And here's the thing: imposter syndrome isn't just a personal quirk—it's a product of environments that weren't exactly designed with us in mind.

You probably know the feeling—you're sitting in a meeting or at a conference, surrounded by people who all seem so confident, so sure of themselves. Meanwhile, you're secretly wondering if you're about to be "found out." Despite your qualifications, experience, and all the hard work you've put in, that doubt creeps in. It's like an internal dialogue that undermines your confidence and holds you back from reaching your full potential.

But here's what I want you to know: imposter syndrome doesn't just stem from insecurity—it's deeply rooted in the systemic issues we've been chatting about.

Early in her career, Kate Maxwell, Worldwide Education Industry executive at Microsoft,[30] felt the sting of self-doubt big time when she found an anonymous note left on her desk one day. It read, "You don't belong here." Can you imagine? That note didn't just hurt—it shook her to her core. "It completely imploded my confidence," she shared. "It led to a tough period that impacted both my work and my life." But here's the silver lining: that experience became a turning point. Maxwell reached out to friends, mentors, a therapist, and even a career coach. Through their support, she rebuilt not just her confidence but her resilience.

"Now I know who I am, I know my worth, and I do not attach my self-worth to the opinions of others," she told me. While she wouldn't wish that experience on anyone, she's grateful for what she learned from it. Maxwell's journey is a powerful reminder that while imposter syndrome can be painful, it's possible to overcome it. With self-validation, external support, and a hefty dose of resilience, imposter syndrome can even become a source of strength and growth.

So, how do we start battling this inner critic? It begins with recognizing that imposter syndrome is common, especially among high achievers.[31] You're not alone in feeling this way. Simply acknowledging these feelings can lessen their power over you.

Next, challenge the doubts in your mind. When that nagging voice says, "You're not qualified," counter it with, "I have the skills and experience to succeed." Replace self-doubt with self-affirmation.

Consider the approach of Penelope Prett, a Fortune 500 executive[32] with over 30 years of experience. Despite being consistently rated as excellent and sought after by clients, Prett would wake up thinking, "Is today the day I get fired?" Even at the height of her career, imposter syndrome was a constant companion. To overcome these feelings, she developed a simple yet effective strategy: focus on facts, not emotions. "When those thoughts come up," she says, "I ask myself, 'When did someone last tell you that you weren't good at your job?' The answer was always never." By grounding herself in reality, Prett was able to push past self-doubt and focus on her next big move.

A thing that's really helped me is keeping a record of my achievements. I jot down my successes—big and small—whenever they happen. So when self-doubt starts creeping in, I can flip back through and remind myself of how far I've come. It's like having a tangible boost right there in my hands to combat those negative thoughts.

And then there always people ready to support you. Connect with mentors, trusted colleagues, or support groups. Sharing your experiences in a safe space can help you gain perspective and feel less isolated. Sometimes just talking about it lifts a weight off your shoulders.[33]

Remember that nobody knows everything, and it's okay to ask questions and acknowledge areas where you're still learning. Give yourself permission to be a work in progress. Taking on challenges is one of the best ways to build confidence. Instead of seeing stepping outside your comfort zone as a threat, think of it as a chance to grow. Every new challenge you tackle adds to your confidence and expands your abilities. Kathryn Guarini, former Chief Information Officer of IBM,[34] encourages women to push their boundaries, saying, "Don't be afraid to take on new roles that might be outside your comfort zone. It's where you learn the most." Her advice reminds us that facing imposter syndrome often means leaning into those intimidating opportunities where real growth happens.

Celebrate your wins, no matter how small they may seem. Take time to acknowledge and appreciate your accomplishments. You deserve to recognize your hard work.

Practicing self-compassion is also key. Be kind to yourself. Treat yourself with the same understanding and support you would offer a friend. Cut yourself some slack; you're doing great.

Changing the narrative in your head can make a big difference. Remind yourself:

"I am enough just as I am."
"I have earned my seat at the table."
"I belong in tech, and my contributions matter."
"I embrace my strengths and celebrate my achievements."
"I am worthy of recognition and praise."
"I am capable of achieving great things."
"I am in control of my own success."
"I deserve my position and the success that comes with it."

Incorporate these affirmations into your daily routine. Over time, they'll help rewire your thinking. And if you still find yourself full of doubt, an executive or career coach can help you identify your barriers, and address them productively head on.

Here's the bottom line: you belong in every room you enter. No one else gets to define your worth. Stand tall, own your space, and don't let anyone—especially that inner critic—convince you otherwise.

Limiting Beliefs: Breaking Free from the Script

A big part of imposter syndrome comes from the limiting beliefs we've been fed—sometimes outright, sometimes in subtle ways—throughout our lives. From a young age, many of us were taught to be modest, to not take up too much space, to second-guess our abilities. These beliefs can hold us back from chasing big opportunities, negotiating for what we're worth, or even speaking up when we know we're right.

I remember chatting with Grace Pérez, former Chief Digital Program Officer, GE HealthCare, who said, "For years, I believed I had to be perfect at everything before I could even consider going for a leadership role. I thought I needed to check every single on the list of requirements, while my male colleagues would just go for it, even if they only ticked a few. It took me a long time to unlearn that conditioning." Pérez's story is one I've heard so many times—women holding themselves back because we've been taught that being good isn't enough; we have to be perfect.

This kind of conditioning is tough to shake, but it's definitely possible. It starts with recognizing those limiting beliefs for what they are—barriers we can dismantle. We've been told to stay in the background, but we have every right to step into the spotlight.

Lack of Role Models: Feeling Alone at the Top

We need to talk about role models—or the lack thereof. One reason imposter syndrome is so pervasive among women in tech is that we don't always see people who look like us in the roles we aspire to. If you don't see women in leadership positions, it's easy to start wondering if you belong there at all.

In an industry dominated by names like Elon Musk and Mark Zuckerberg, women leaders like Mary Barra and Mira Murati are still the exceptions rather than the rule. If you need more proof that the tech world is overwhelmingly male, just take a look at Investopedia's list of "The 10 Richest People in the World.[35]" All ten are men, and eight of them are tech leaders. That scarcity of female role models makes a huge difference. When you don't see people who look like you at the top, you start to wonder whether there's a path for you at all. And this isn't just a challenge for women at the beginning of their careers—it's something even seasoned executives struggle with. In a world where social media dominates our lives, young girls don't often see women at the forefront of tech and think, "I want to be her when I grow up."

One executive shared: "I spent years looking around for someone like me in the C-suite, and when I didn't find anyone, I started to wonder if I was aiming too high. It's hard to shake that feeling of isolation, even when you're surrounded by colleagues. It's like you're always second-guessing yourself because there's no one who's walked the same path."

The reality is, when you're the only woman—or one of a few—in the room, the pressure is intense. You're not just representing yourself; you feel like you're representing all women. That kind of pressure can feed into the cycle of self-doubt that fuels imposter syndrome.

This process of unlearning and reconditioning takes time. It's about reclaiming the narrative and recognizing that you deserve to be in the room—not because you've checked every box, but because your presence is valuable in itself.

Turning Barriers into Fuel

One of the most important tools you can use to overcome these barriers is resilience—a topic we'll explore in depth in Chapter 8. As Reetal Pai, Executive Vice President, Chief Information Officer at Teichert[36] said, "Resilience is about bouncing back from setbacks...it's a crucial skill in tech." Every time you face bias or a challenge, you have the opportunity to grow stronger and more determined. In the tech industry, where challenges are a given—whether it's being overlooked for a promotion, dealing with microaggressions, or navigating imposter syndrome—resilience is what will keep you moving forward. It's about turning those obstacles into fuel for your own progress, using them to push ahead when the path feels blocked.

Each setback becomes a learning experience, an opportunity to pivot, and a moment to build strength. The more resilient you become, the better equipped you are to handle whatever comes your way. As a matter of fact, an overwhelming 95% of executives acknowledge that resilience has become increasingly important as they've advanced in their careers.[37] This mindset helps women in tech not just survive but thrive in environments that can be tough to navigate.

But it's not just about breaking through for yourself.

Every time you succeed, you make it easier for someone else to follow. Daphne E. Jones, former Chief Information Officer at GE HealthCare Global Services,[38] captured this sentiment perfectly: "My role is to empower the underserved, the overlooked, the undervalued, the underestimated." Every victory chips away at the barriers for those who come next, and that's how real change happens. By overcoming these challenges, you're not just creating a path for yourself—you're paving the way for others who may have felt they didn't belong or didn't have the chance to succeed.

Each of us has a role to play in making tech more inclusive, more equitable, and more welcoming to those who've been traditionally left out. Empowering yourself is the first step, but empowering others is how we create lasting change. Every barrier you break down helps those who come after you, making the tech industry a little more open, a little more diverse, and a lot more powerful.

We've covered a lot in this chapter—from the gender leadership gap and systemic biases to how imposter syndrome creeps. It's a lot to take in, but here's the key message I want you to walk away with: these barriers, as overwhelming as they may seem, can also be your fuel.

Every obstacle you face is an opportunity to grow stronger, more resilient, and more determined to succeed. The gender leadership gap might persist, but that doesn't mean you can't be part of the solution. And remember, you don't have to do it alone. Lean on your allies, find mentors, and build a support system that helps you succeed, both in and outside of work. Advocate for yourself, and don't be afraid to speak up when something feels wrong. The more we talk about these issues, the more we can dismantle the systems that keep women out of leadership roles.

Looking ahead, this book will focus on practical strategies for overcoming these barriers. From building your personal brand to finding the right mentors, we'll explore actionable steps you can take to not just survive in tech, but thrive. Because your voice matters. Your contributions matter. And the tech industry needs you—your ideas, your leadership, and your perspective.

So let's break through these barriers together and start shaping the future of tech, not just one woman at a time, but one team at a time, one department at a time, and one company at a time—creating a positive snowball effect that can reshape the tech industry.

- **Transform Barriers into Growth:** Challenges can fuel resilience. How can you turn recent setbacks into learning opportunities?
- **Reframe Imposter Syndrome:** 70% of people experience self-doubt. Use it as a sign you're pushing boundaries. What recent doubts signal growth for you?
- **Unlearn Limiting Beliefs:** What subconscious beliefs are holding you back, and how can you replace them with affirmations of your worth?
- **Embrace Imperfection:** Men apply for roles with only 60% of qualifications.[39] How can you step outside your comfort zone today?
- **Be a Role Model:** Even if role models are scarce, your journey can inspire others. Who looks up to you, and how can you empower them?

2

Shaping Your Journey in Tech

We need to accept that we won't always make the right decisions, that we'll screw up royally sometimes—understanding that failure is not the opposite of success, it's part of success.

—Arianna Huffington

Have you ever been asked, "Where do you see yourself in five years?" It's a classic career question that can feel both exciting and intimidating. For some, the answer comes naturally, filled with ambition and clarity. But for others, the question can spark a swirl of possibilities and even uncertainty. Maybe you're thriving in your role yet still feel the tug of something more. Or perhaps you're at a crossroads, wondering if the path you're on will lead to the impact you want to make.

The goal of this chapter is to explore practical techniques and tools for shaping a distinct and fulfilling career in technology. We'll delve into building self-awareness, aligning your career with your core values, setting and reassessing your goals, and preparing for those pivotal moments that can redefine your path.

Building Self-Awareness and Career Identity

From my personal experiences, in-depth interviews with global tech leaders and supporting studies,[1] I've learned that self-awareness is a key pillar supporting a successful and meaningful career. In practice, self-awareness is built on connecting with your values, strengths, and motivations, and using these as a foundation to make intentional career moves.

Ivneet Kaur, EVP and Chief Information and Technology Officer at Sterling,[2] emphasized the importance of self-awareness when I asked her about self-reflection in personal and professional growth. "I wish I had that self-awareness sooner," she said. "Finding what you're good at helps you find your purpose and move forward. It's important to believe in yourself and your abilities." Her words highlight the resilience and confidence that come with self-awareness, allowing us to navigate challenges with grace.

Kaur shared how yoga has played a crucial role in boosting her self-awareness and leadership style. She mentioned, "Practices like understanding different perspectives, seeking to understand before being understood, and staying calm in difficult situations without reacting impulsively have been invaluable." This insight emphasizes the continuous journey of self-awareness and its significant impact on personal growth and leadership.

So, how do you cultivate self-awareness? Start with a practice that feels right for you—it could be journaling, meditation, engaging in mindful listening, practicing gratitude, exploring creative activities, or something else.

For me, self-awareness started when I began taking time to reflect. I kept a journal, jotting down my thoughts, feelings, and reactions to different experiences at work. Using apps like Day One or the Five Minute Journal, which allow you to capture moods and specific reflections, made it easy to turn this into a sustainable habit. Over time, this practice helped me see patterns—what work genuinely excited me and what left me feeling drained.

Examples:

- I spent most of the day updating spreadsheets and handling administrative tasks. Found myself feeling drained and checking the clock often. Administrative work seems to sap my energy. I need an assistant urgently!

- I gave a presentation at a conference. Was nervous beforehand but received positive feedback afterward. Felt a strong sense of accomplishment and realized I enjoy public speaking more than I thought. I should do it more often!

Another powerful way I built self-awareness was by seeking feedback from others. I started asking colleagues and mentors for honest insights about my strengths and areas where I could grow. If asking directly feels awkward or a bit uncomfortable, consider using a written format. Tools like Google Forms, Typeform, or SurveyMonkey allow you to collect structured, anonymous feedback.

This feedback acted like an external mirror—revealing qualities I had overlooked, highlighting skills others valued in me that I hadn't fully recognized, and pointing out areas for improvement I wasn't aware of. Though sometimes hard to hear, these insights were invaluable, giving me a fresh perspective on myself as a leader.

Mindfulness became an unexpected ally for me. Setting aside just a few minutes each day for meditation helped me tune into my thoughts and feelings. For you, it might be taking a walk in nature, practicing deep-breathing exercises, or mindful eating—whatever helps you connect with the present moment. According to a study[3] by Harvard researchers, mindfulness practice can actually change brain structures associated with learning, memory, and emotional regulation. The American Psychological Association[4] also notes that mindfulness meditation reduces stress and improves attention. Apps like Serenity, Headspace, or Calm can help you create a habit through a guided process. Mindfulness doesn't mean finding answers right away; instead, it gives you the space to listen to your inner voice without distraction. Simple but consistent practices like mindful listening during meetings and taking intentional pauses between tasks or back-to-back meetings can help clear your mind.

I also started incorporating a simple gratitude practice into my daily routine. Before going to sleep, I'd ask myself, "What am I grateful for today?" I'd take a moment to acknowledge three things I was thankful for that day—a successful product launch, a breakthrough in a challenging project, a supportive conversation with a colleague, sharing a meal with family, enjoying a beautiful sunset, or even appreciating a moment of laughter with friends.

Self-awareness might sound abstract, but it's a deeply practical foundation for building a career that feels genuine. It's what allows us to make intentional decisions that reflect our true identity rather than conforming to an external idea of "success." When we know our strengths, values, and motivations, we're better equipped to seek out opportunities that resonate with who we are. We're able to create a career path that doesn't just meet expectations but feels meaningful and aligned.

An ancient proverb says: "If you don't have time to meditate for an hour each day, then you should meditate for two." In modern terms, this means that the busier we are, the more we benefit from moments of pause and introspection. Blocking off time to cultivate mindfulness and engage in self-reflective activities can provide the perspective needed to gain clarity.

Aligning Personal Values with Career Decisions

Years ago, I reached a point where I had to ask myself, "Am I doing this because it's what I'm good at, or because it's what I love?" I'd been exploring various directions, taking on roles and projects that challenged me. But it wasn't until I aligned my work with my core values—inclusion, empowerment, and impact—that I found a deeper sense of fulfillment. My career shifted from being a checklist of milestones to a path that truly reflected who I am and the difference I want to make.

Seeing the lack of representation and opportunities for women in tech and leadership, I felt a strong urge to take action, leading to creating WomenTech Network. Inclusion meant creating spaces where everyone, regardless of gender, could feel welcomed and valued. Empowerment was about providing the tools and support women needed to thrive in a male-dominated field. Impact drove me to strive for meaningful change that would resonate beyond individual careers and influence the industry as a whole.

In an interview, Aysha Khan, CISO and CIO of Treasure Data,[5] shared her reflections on values with me. She said, "I have absolute clarity about my life, who I am, and what I want to be. I know why I'm here on this planet in this space and time. I know my mission. My top three values are connections, impact, and inner peace. I've done a lot of self-reflection and spent time asking myself these questions. Connections: Family, meaningful conversations, and soulful relationships. Impact: I am not doing it for a paycheck; I am doing it to make an impact. Inner Peace: I believe in inner peace."

If you were to list your core values right now, what would they be? It might seem like an abstract exercise but identifying what you genuinely care about can be one of the most powerful tools for aligning your career. For me, understanding my core values didn't happen overnight, and it took a few missteps to uncover what truly drives me. But once I did, these values became a compass for my decisions, giving my career new direction and meaning.

Inspired by Brené Brown's "Dare to Lead,"[6] I began to explore and reassess my own values more intentionally. I started by writing down all the values that resonated with me—anything that felt important. Then I reflected and narrowed down the list, circling those that spoke to me most and challenging myself to pick the top two or three. I asked myself, "Which values are essential to who I am?" Defining how these values manifest in daily life made them more tangible. For example, if courage was a core value, it might involve speaking up in meetings or taking on challenging projects. If compassion was important, it could mean actively listening or offering support to colleagues in need.

What also helped me was reflecting on peak experiences—those moments when I felt truly fulfilled or proud. I asked myself, "What values was I honoring during these times?" I considered as well what angers me, realizing that frustrations often highlight values that feel violated.

In the process, I recognized the importance of identifying misalignments—situations where I wasn't honoring my values—so I could adjust accordingly. Living by your values doesn't mean you'll be perfect; there will be times when you fall short. But being aware allows you to make conscious choices and realign when necessary.

Studies have consistently shown that when individuals perceive a strong fit between their personal values and their organization's values, it leads to higher job satisfaction and greater organizational commitment.[7]

Aligning your values with your career doesn't always require drastic changes like switching jobs. Often, it's about finding ways to bring more of what matters to you into your current role rather than chasing the "perfect" job. If you're in a technical position but value collaboration, you might find fulfillment in cross-functional projects that encourage teamwork. If diversity and inclusion are important to you, perhaps you can advocate for these causes within your organization—maybe by joining or starting an Employee Resource or Affinity Group. When our responsibilities and tasks resonate with our values, we tap into a source of motivation that keeps us engaged and resilient, even when challenges arise.

It's important to acknowledge that core values can evolve as we grow and adapt. Significant life experiences—like personal achievements, losses, or challenges—can lead us to re-evaluate what's most important. Penelope Prett,[8] a Fortune 500 senior executive, experienced this firsthand. A severe illness reshaped her approach to both work and life. Before this turning point, she was a "hard charger," rarely stopping to catch her breath. After her recovery, she committed to finding joy in every step of her journey. "Same work, different approach," she explained. This shift helped her align her career with a deeper sense of purpose, showing that clarity often comes when we look beyond conventional measures of success and focus on ful- fillment in our daily experiences.

When your career decisions are guided by your values, your work trans- forms into more than just a job—it becomes an authentic expression of your purpose. It's a way to contribute to the world that aligns deeply with who you are, creating an experience that's profoundly meaningful, sustain- able, and uniquely yours.

Setting and Reassessing Goals for Long-Term Fulfillment

When we first start our careers, setting goals often feels straightforward— land that job, learn new skills, aim for promotions, or take on bigger pro- jects. But as our careers evolve, so does our sense of what we truly want. The goals we once chased might not hold the same meaning they used to, and new aspirations can start to emerge. New priorities start to emerge. Achiev- ing one milestone often reveals new dimensions to success, redefining what we're reaching toward. And as I've learned from my own path and from conversations with other leaders in tech, this shifting sense of purpose isn't unusual—it's part of a broader path to finding real fulfillment.

Sometimes, redefining goals feels like a natural next step. Other times, it can be confusing, especially if traditional markers of success—like title changes, salary bumps, or prestigious roles—aren't sparking the same excite- ment they once did. This is when reassessing our goals becomes essential. Allowing ourselves to redefine success makes room for goals that don't just look impressive on a résumé but resonate deeply with our values and aspirations.

Take the story of Asha Keddy, previously a Corporate Vice President at Intel,[9] for example. After achieving significant success in her field, she came to a point where she wanted something more lasting than a job title. She began to prioritize projects that allowed her to give back, to innovate, and to serve a larger purpose. "I want to focus on paying it forward and doing things that have a lasting impact," she shared. Her story is a reminder that even in established careers, it's never too late to pivot toward something that feels more meaningful. For Keddy, success was no longer about reaching a new level; it was about deepening her impact.

Reassessing goals can often reveal new ways to bring purpose into our work. For some, it might mean focusing on mentorship and guiding the next generation of talent. For others, it could involve seeking out roles that enable creative problem-solving, innovation, or even policy influence. By allowing our goals to grow with us, we keep our work feeling relevant and inspiring, avoiding the feeling of simply "going through the motions."

As our goals evolve, career mapping becomes essential for staying connected to what truly matters in our work. It allows us to view our journey with a broader perspective, ensuring each choice aligns with our values and aspirations. Rather than expecting a perfectly linear path—especially in tech, where careers rarely follow straight lines—we create a flexible road map that reflects our authentic goals. Research by Deloitte[10] emphasizes the need to move away from traditional, rigid career ladders in favor of adaptable, skills-based pathways that support continuous growth. By charting these paths, we identify valuable gaps—skills to develop, experiences to seek, or roles to explore—that prepare us for the challenges ahead.

For example, if you're a senior engineering manager with aspirations toward a strategic leadership role like CTO, career mapping can help identify growth areas aligned with CTO responsibilities. These might include strategic technology planning, cross-departmental collaboration, and understanding business impact. You could set goals to lead cross-functional projects involving product, data, and design teams to gain experience in high-level decision-making. Gaining exposure to budgeting, vendor management, and long-term tech strategy can be also crucial.

Visualizing these insights with tools like MindMeister, Miro, or Mural can be incredibly helpful. They allow you to create digital mind maps around your values, strengths, and long-term goals, turning complex ideas into clear, organized visuals. If you prefer a more structured approach, Notion integrates mind maps with daily reflections, career planning, and habit tracking—all in one place. Visualizing our thoughts makes abstract ideas tangible, helping us see the connections between our values and goals and clarifying what comes next.

Finally, regularly reviewing our goals ensures they stay aligned with our evolving values and priorities. This isn't losing focus—it's refining it, a sign of growth. As our aspirations shift toward personal impact, our goals should reflect who we are now and where we want to go. This alignment turns our achievements into meaningful milestones, making career mapping a fulfilling path toward the future.

Navigating Leadership Pivot Points

Throughout my career and in conversations with leaders across tech, I've come to realize that pivot points are often the biggest drivers of growth—they're turning points that define us.

I was talking to Deborah Corwin Scott,[11] former CIO at Harvard Medical School, who's navigated multiple career transitions. Reflecting on her journey, she shared, "One of the biggest pivots was moving from managing technology to managing people. It was tough," she admitted. "I realized I was no longer the expert with my hands on the keyboard. I had to let go of control and focus on leadership." Corwin Scott described this transition as a significant shift—from completing tasks to developing people. It required embracing new ways of communicating, providing effective feedback, and fostering a collaborative environment.

Whether stepping up from an individual contributor to a manager, moving into a director role, or aiming for the executive suite, each transition brings its own challenges and opportunities.

From Individual Contributor to Manager

One of the most significant shifts in a tech career is moving from being an individual contributor to becoming a manager. It's a coveted step, but many of us struggle with letting go of control. As a manager, you need to trust your team to handle tasks you once managed yourself. This can be challenging, especially if you're used to being hands-on.

I remember when I first made this transition. I wanted to dive into every detail to ensure everything was done "right." But I quickly realized this approach wasn't sustainable. Not only was I burning myself out, but

I was also hindering my team's growth by not giving them space to develop their own skills.

To navigate this transition, I started scheduling regular one-on-one meetings with my team members. These check-ins helped me understand their goals and challenges, and how I could support them better. It wasn't just about project updates; it was about building relationships and trust.

I also continued journaling, focusing on reflections about my leadership style. I'd ask myself questions like, "How did I handle that situation?" or "Did I give my team enough autonomy today?" This self-reflection helped me identify areas where I could improve as a leader.

Investing time in learning was crucial. I took courses on team development and communication. One resource I highly recommend is Julie Zhuo's book, *The Making of a Manager*.[12] Julie began her career at Facebook as an intern and was promoted to her first managerial role by 25. She wrote, "All that I knew of management could be neatly summarized into two words: meetings and PROMOTION. I mean, this was a promotion, wasn't it?" Her belief that "great managers are made, not born" resonated with me. It reassured me that even if I didn't feel like a natural-born manager, I could develop the skills needed.

Those first 90 days as a new manager are often very intense. You might feel super stressed and, at times, lost about your new role. But by focusing on building relationships, seeking feedback, and investing in your growth you will begin to find your footing.

If you're currently an individual contributor but see yourself in a leadership role, start by seeking opportunities that allow for collaboration and mentorship. Volunteer to lead projects, take initiative in team settings, and build relationships with others in management. Consider finding a mentor who can guide you, share their own experiences, and help you develop your leadership skills.

From Manager to Director

Stepping up from managing a team to managing managers is often the next significant leap. Instead of just overseeing people, now you are leading through others and shaping a bigger picture. At this stage, you're expected to think beyond daily tasks and focus on long-term vision, strategy, and team dynamics at a higher level.

Asha Keddy shared how this pivot came with challenges. "They said, 'Either you change, or we will quit.' I knew something had to change," she admitted. "I had just become a manager of managers and was still applying the skills I learned from leading individual contributors. I was also a micro-manager. My transition was rough."

She continued, "I started to ask for feedback from the managers I led on how I could improve. Through time, trial and error, listening, and learning from their feedback, I became an effective second-line manager."

The promotion to a director role often means you have to manage managers—leaders like the one you were yesterday. The most challenging aspect is that a director's expectations are often vague, and there's typically no preparation for handling the day-to-day responsibilities of the new role.

I faced similar challenges as my responsibilities grew. I realized that delegation became even more critical. I began assigning ownership of projects to my managers, focusing on outcomes rather than processes. This shift allowed them to develop their own leadership styles and take full responsibility for their teams.

I also found value in visualizing our strategic goals and mapping out the vision across different teams, ensuring alignment and clarity where we were going and how each team contributed to the larger picture.

Seeking mentorship was another crucial step. I connected with someone experienced in managing managers. Their insights on scaling leadership skills and empowering others were invaluable. We'll explore more about mentorship in Chapter 5.

You might be wondering, how do you know when you're ready to make this leap? Some signs include having the capacity to focus on strategy, successfully managing teams, running productive meetings, knowing how to hire top talent (and when to let people go), and being able to support and coach managers effectively.

McKinsey's insights[13] highlight four key behaviors that successful upper management leaders tend to master: problem-solving, results orientation, gathering diverse perspectives, and providing supportive guidance. At this level, directors excel by aligning cross-functional teams and strategically guiding their managers, moving from managing tasks to orchestrating outcomes on a larger scale.

But don't worry if you don't tick all the boxes. Everyone's journey is unique, and it's normal to feel you may not be completely ready.

What's important is your willingness to learn and grow. Don't let perfectionism hold you back. Believe in your potential and take that leap even if you don't feel fully prepared.

If you're a manager aiming to move into a director role, focus on developing a strategic mindset. Look for projects that require thinking about long-term impact, resource allocation, and cross-functional collaboration. Practice delegation, invest time in developing your team's leaders, and learn how to prioritize on a broader scale. These steps will help you succeed in this new role.

From Director to Vice President (VP)

At this level, your decisions don't just impact your direct reports or your department—they shape the entire organization. As McKinsey[14] notes, this shift involves balancing immediate operational needs with a longer-term vision, often under increased scrutiny.

Fern Johnson, former CTO and Vice President of Infrastructure & Operations at PepsiCo,[15] described the shift to VP as a "complete mindset change." Transitioning into an executive role required her to prioritize across multiple departments, manage conflicting needs, and think cross-functionally. "I had to shift from managing specific projects to creating alignment across the organization," she shared. This meant building alliances with other leaders, understanding the company's broader strategic goals, fostering collaboration, and influencing culture.

In this role, leadership becomes less about immediate details and more about vision and legacy. You're balancing short-term needs with long-term impact, taking on stewardship for the company's future. Communication becomes even more critical. Maintaining clear and open channels with the CEO, other executives, and your teams is essential. This level challenges you to develop resilience, as choices come with greater responsibility and impact. But it's also an opportunity to shape the organization's direction, influence company culture, and create lasting impact.

As you move closer to executive roles, focus on developing skills in cross-functional leadership, strategic alignment, and cultural influence. Building relationships across departments and fostering alliances with other leaders to create a unified vision is crucial.

From Vice President to Chief (C-level)

Transitioning to a C-level or chief role brings an entirely new set of responsibilities and expectations. You're no longer just shaping company policy—you're the guardian of the organization's vision, values, and reputation. The impact at this level is immense, requiring agility, vision, and a commitment to nurturing a culture of resilience and innovation.

Kathryn Guarini, former Chief Information Officer at IBM,[16] shared her experiences stepping into the CIO role, describing how she faced a steep learning curve. "When I took on the role at IBM, there was a lot I didn't know about the scope of it. I didn't know the team, the portfolio of responsibilities, the priorities, or how to manage critical situations. There was so much to learn, and it was exciting to me. But it's also challenging because you're in a leadership role with massive responsibility," she recalled. In this role, Guarini had to adapt quickly, build new relationships, and make critical decisions that affected the entire organization. Usually, success at this level means creating a culture of trust, accountability, and continuous improvement across teams. Transitioning to a C-level role is as much about influencing and inspiring as it is about making decisions. It's about setting the tone for the organization and ensuring the company's values are reflected at every level.

Another example is Linda Yao's[17] path to becoming the Chief Operating Officer and Head of Strategy, Solutions & Services Group at Lenovo. Her journey was anything but typical. She started her career in finance, working in banking and mergers and acquisitions. Her passion for aviation led her to Boeing, where she built a data science arm and later moved again into a merger and acquisitions role. Each step was a calculated leap into the unknown, driven by a love for learning and a willingness to embrace discomfort.

"For me, the path to C-suite was unconventional," Yao shares. "Despite my lack of direct operations experience, I had always embraced roles that stretched my abilities and placed me outside my comfort zone. The key to my transition was relying heavily on the expertise of my team and providing them with two things: air cover to execute their vision and the necessary support to make it happen."

She further emphasizes that being a great leader often means being the "dumbest person in the room," surrounding yourself with experts, and empowering them to excel.

When I stepped into a C-level role, understanding who the key stakeholders were and how they influenced the organization was crucial. Prioritizing these relationships and communication channels made a significant difference.

Implementing feedback channels became essential. I encouraged anonymous input to gain insights into team perception and culture, helping me adjust strategies and address concerns proactively.

Considering executive coaching was another step I took. Having someone provide customized advice on resilience, decision-making, and influence was invaluable. It offered a sounding board and challenged me to think differently.

To help succeed in such transitions, applying frameworks like *The First 90 Days* by Michael D. Watkins[18] can be beneficial. But it's also important to recognize the unique challenges faced by women in leadership roles. Navigating these transitions requires not just strategic acumen but also resilience, adaptability, and a strong support network.

If you're preparing for a C-level role, focus on cultivating resilience, adaptability, and the ability to lead through complexity. This pivot will likely demand balancing innovation with stability and vision with operational execution. Building a network of trusted advisors, staying open to feedback, and nurturing a strong sense of purpose will serve you well as you take on a role that requires both influence and adaptability.

Each pivot challenges you to grow, expand your abilities, and deepen your impact. When approached thoughtfully, these transitions become meaningful steps toward a career that advances you professionally and reflects your true self.

With a strong foundation of self-awareness, aligned values, and meaningful goals, the next step is sharing your journey with others. In the next chapter, we'll explore how to craft a personal brand that resonates with your identity and shares your vision with the world. By combining inner awareness with external visibility, you'll be ready to engage with the tech industry—and the world—with confidence, clarity, and authenticity.

- **Cultivate Self-Awareness**: Reflecting on your values, strengths, and motivations is foundational. What daily practices can you adopt to deepen your understanding of yourself?
- **Align Career with Core Values**: 80%[19] of professionals feel more engaged when their work aligns with their values. What are your top three core values, and how do they manifest in your career choices?
- **Set and Reassess Goals**: As you evolve, so do your aspirations. Are your current goals aligned with who you are today and who you want to become?
- **Prepare for Pivot Points**: Career transitions are opportunities for growth. What skills or experiences do you need to acquire to navigate your next pivot successfully?
- **Seek Feedback**: Honest feedback can act as a mirror to reveal unseen strengths and areas for improvement. Who can you approach for constructive insights to aid your development?
- **Practice Mindfulness and Gratitude**: Incorporating mindfulness can reduce stress by up to 30%.[20] How can you integrate mindfulness and gratitude into your daily routine to enhance well-being and leadership effectiveness?

3

Building and Growing Your Personal Brand

I had no idea that being your authentic self could make me as rich as I've become. If I had, I'd have done it a lot earlier.

—Oprah Winfrey

While writing this book, I've been thinking a lot about how we define ourselves. If your job title and company affiliation disappeared tomorrow, who would you be? What would people remember about you? Your personal brand is that story—it's what remains when everything else is stripped away. It's the reputation that opens doors and the impression that lingers long after you've left the room.

When you hear "personal brand," maybe you think about your LinkedIn profile or how you present yourself in meetings. And sure, that's part of it. But it's so much more than that. It's how you show up in every aspect of your life—the unique blend of your skills, experiences, and personality that shapes how others perceive you. It's not just about what you do; it's about who you are at your core.

Having a strong personal brand isn't just a nice-to-have; it's essential. Did you know that a national study by the Brand Builders Group[1] shows that 74% of Americans are more likely to trust someone with an established personal brand? Plus, 82% agree that companies are more influential if their executives have a personal brand they know and follow. That's pretty significant!

Despite this, many professionals fall into the trap of assuming that good work will speak for itself. We focus on daily tasks, hoping our contributions will get noticed. But in reality, great work isn't enough if no one knows about it. Building your brand requires deliberate effort—highlighting not just what you've achieved, but also the unique value you bring to the table.

Through my own journey, I realized that personal branding isn't about creating a persona or fitting into someone else's mold. It's about being intentional and authentic. To simplify the process, I developed this formula:

Personal Brand = (Authenticity + Expertise) ⋆ Visibility

This formula underscores the dynamic interplay between these elements:

- Authenticity is about staying true to who you are—your values, personality, and journey. It fosters trust and relatability, making connections deeper and more meaningful.
- Expertise reflects your knowledge, skills, and accomplishments. It builds credibility and positions you as a reliable professional or thought leader in your field.
- Visibility is the multiplier. It amplifies your authenticity and expertise, ensuring your value is recognized by the right people. Without visibility, even the most authentic and skilled individuals can remain overlooked.

The weight of these elements may shift depending on where you are in your career or your specific goals:

- **Early Career:** Visibility often takes precedence as you work to get noticed and establish connections.
- **Leadership Roles:** Authenticity becomes critical for building trust and inspiring teams.

■ **Specialized Fields**: Expertise is paramount for demonstrating authority and depth in your niche.

Recognizing how these factors interact and tailoring your efforts accordingly can maximize your impact.

Let's explore how authenticity and expertise contribute to this formula (Table 3.1):

Table 3.1 Authenticity Versus Expertise

Aspect	Authenticity	Expertise
Definition	Staying true to your values, personality, and journey.	Showcasing skills, knowledge, and accomplishments that define your strengths.
Purpose	Builds trust and relatability, creating genuine connections.	Establishes credibility and positions you as a knowledgeable professional.
Core Practices	• Practicing self-reflection • Sharing personal stories and values • Consistency	• Continuous learning • Highlighting key achievements • Sharing insights
Benefits	• Encourages trust and loyalty • Makes you memorable and unique	• Demonstrates authority • Increases opportunities for recognition and growth
Risks	Risk of oversharing or being seen as unprofessional if boundaries aren't clear.	Risk of appearing distant or overly polished if authenticity is neglected.
Perception	"Relatable and trustworthy—someone I can connect with."	"Skilled and competent—a leader who delivers results."
Balance Strategy	Use authenticity to share your journey, motivations, and setbacks.	Use expertise to reinforce authenticity with accomplishments and value.

Visibility ties it all together. It's about ensuring that your authenticity and expertise are seen and recognized. Visibility doesn't mean self-promotion for its own sake—it means strategically sharing your story, achievements, and values with the right audience. Whether it's through social media, networking, or public speaking, visibility ensures your personal brand creates the impact it deserves.

Personal branding is a continual process of learning, refining, and connecting. Not everyone will resonate with your brand—and that's okay. What matters is aligning it with your goals and reaching the people who value what you bring to the table.

As we explore this formula further, think about your own journey. How are you showing up authentically? How are you demonstrating your expertise? And most importantly, how visible are you to the people who can help you achieve your goals?

Authenticity

I wouldn't blame you if you rolled your eyes every time you heard the word *authenticity*, but it's more than a buzzword. At its core, authenticity is about being true to who you are, even as you adapt to different environments. It's the ability to show up as your whole self, without feeling the need to conform to someone else's expectations in ways that compromise your core values.[2] While it's natural to adjust your approach depending on the context—whether you're in the boardroom or at the dinner table with friends—authenticity means maintaining consistency in your values, integrity, and sense of self across these different settings.

Why is authenticity so crucial in personal branding? Because trust thrives when authenticity is present, as people are naturally drawn to those who show up with sincerity and integrity. When individuals present themselves honestly, they project transparency and invite connection. Kathryn Guarini, the former CIO at IBM,[3] shared her thoughts on authenticity in leadership. She reflected, "One of the key aspects that has evolved for me is being extremely transparent and authentic. While I've always strived to be genuine, I now believe that trying to appear perfect doesn't benefit anyone. I've achieved many things in my life and career, and I'm not afraid to acknowledge that, but I also openly admit that I don't have all the answers."

Guarini's experience highlights a critical point: authenticity isn't about pretending to be perfect; it's about embracing your strengths and acknowledging your weaknesses. It's about showing up as your true self—not a polished version you think others want to see. This kind of honesty not only builds trust but also fosters deeper connections with those around you.

The Power of Vulnerability

Being authentic also means being open about the challenges you've faced and how you've overcome them. It's tempting to only share your successes, but the reality is, people connect more deeply when you are also honest about your struggles. Sharing these experiences makes you relatable—it shows that you're human, just like everyone else.

Janet Robertson, Global CIO at RS Group,[4] shared a powerful story about how she embraced transparency during a particularly challenging time. "Interestingly enough, it was way into COVID when it really changed for me dramatically. I had two employees take their lives during the pandemic, and that's when I realized that not being real about what I was going through at the time with my team was doing them a disservice. That was a big one. There's a level of professionalism that…you can be who you are and be a real person. It doesn't take away your authority or your power to be human."

Robertson's experience marked a turning point in her leadership style. She recognized that by being more transparent about her personal struggles, she could connect with her team on a deeper level. This wasn't just about being a more relatable leader; it was also about creating a culture where her team felt safe to be open about their own challenges. In the midst of a global crisis, this level of authenticity wasn't just beneficial—it was necessary.

Practical Ways to Embrace Authenticity

So, how do you actually live out authenticity in your personal brand? It's not about adopting a new strategy overnight; it's about making small, intentional changes that reflect who you truly are, both in and out of the workplace.

Self-Reflection   We discussed self-reflection in Chapter 2 for building self-awareness and career advancement. When it comes to authenticity it can further help you understand who you are and what you stand for to help you build your personal brand.

In a conversation with a good friend of mine who had recently taken on a new leadership role, she shared with me, "I felt like I needed to be a different person—more authoritative, less approachable—because that's what I thought leadership demanded. But the more I tried to fit that mold, the more I felt disconnected from my team and even from myself." We talked about the moments when she felt most connected to her work and her team, and she realized it was when she was open and approachable, not when she tried to be someone she wasn't. From that moment, she decided to lean into those strengths, even if it didn't fit the traditional image of a leader.

Brand Consistency   It doesn't mean being rigid or unchanging but rather ensuring that who you are in one context matches who you are in another. Picture this: You're at a company-wide meeting, and you've prepared to present a new idea. You're confident in small group settings but tend to hold back in larger forums, afraid of being judged. After the meeting, a colleague mentions that you seemed reserved, which surprises them because they've seen how dynamic you are in smaller meetings. This is a moment of realization—are you consistently showing up as your true self, regardless of the setting?

To address it, think about how you can bring that same energy and authenticity from small meetings into larger settings. It might involve reminding yourself before a big meeting that your ideas are just as valuable in a large room as they are in a one-on-one. Or maybe it's about finding ways to interact with your audience during the presentation, turning it into a conversation rather than a monologue. Such a strategy can help you maintain that consistent, authentic presence.

Storytelling   Oftentimes, the connotation of sharing your story is misunderstood as oversharing every detail of your life. However, it truly means being open about the challenges and triumphs that have shaped you. Take a moment to think about a time when you overcame a significant obstacle. What did you learn from that experience? How did it change the way you approach your work or your interactions with others?

Imagine sharing that story in a mentoring session or a team meeting. Instead of focusing solely on the outcome, talk about the process—what it felt like to navigate uncertainty, the moments of doubt, and how you pushed through. This not only humanizes you but also makes you relatable. It shows that you're not just a leader or a colleague; you're a person who has faced and overcome challenges, just like everyone else (Table 3.2).

Table 3.2   Storytelling Formats for Leaders

Storytelling Format	Description	Example
1. Defining Moments Approach	Focus on key turning points in your career or life that led to significant lessons or changes in perspective.	"One of my defining moments was when I was assigned to a struggling project. I realized that leadership was less about having all the answers and more about empowering my team."
2. Hero's Journey Framework	Frame your story as a journey where you face challenges, learn valuable lessons, and emerge transformed.	"When I transitioned from a manager to a director, I struggled with imposter syndrome. Embracing my unique strengths made me a more confident and empathetic leader."
3. Values-Driven Narrative	Highlight how your core values have guided your decisions and actions over time.	"Integrity has always been my guiding value. Early on, I made a tough but principled decision that earned trust and set the tone for my leadership style."
4. Mentor and Guide Format	Focus on influential mentors or guides who have shaped your journey, showcasing humility and the value of learning from others.	"I've had mentors who taught me the power of empathy and resilience. Their lessons have profoundly shaped how I lead and tackle challenges with my team."

(continued)

Table 3.2 (*Continued*)

Storytelling Format	Description	Example
5. Crossroads Approach	Discuss critical decision points where choices shaped your future path and the lessons learned.	"At a turning point in my career, I left a stable role for a challenging opportunity. Choosing growth over comfort really shaped where I am today."
6. Industry Evolution Perspective	Share how you've adapted to industry changes over time, highlighting your adaptability and forward-thinking approach.	"When I started in tech, AI used to feel like science fiction. Now, it's part of my everyday work. Diving into machine learning was challenging, but it's thrilling to be at the forefront of technology that's changing the world."

Vulnerability   This can be one of the most challenging aspects of authenticity, especially in a professional setting where there's often pressure to appear strong and unflappable. But vulnerability is where true connection happens.

Think about a time when you were struggling with a project or a decision and felt the need to keep those doubts to yourself. Now, imagine how things might have been different if you had shared those doubts with a trusted colleague or mentor. Maybe you would have received valuable advice or simply felt less isolated in your experience. By opening up about your struggles, you create space for others to do the same, fostering a culture of openness and trust.[5]

Consider this scenario: You're leading a project, and things aren't going as planned. Instead of trying to maintain a façade of control, you decide to have an honest conversation with your team. "I don't have a clear solution right now," you might say, "and I'd really value your input." This not only shows your team that you trust and respect their perspectives but also models authentic leadership. It's a powerful way to bring your whole self to your role. Another example could be not trying to be the smartest person in the room: "This project touches on some areas that I'm less familiar with, so I'd love to lean on those of you with experience here. I'm here to learn, too."

Owning up to mistakes is another powerful form of vulnerability in leadership. When a decision doesn't go as planned, acknowledging it openly shows that you as a leader are not trying to avoid accountability. Instead, by saying something like, "In hindsight, that wasn't the right call, and I take responsibility for it. I'd love your input on how we can adjust moving forward," a leader invites collaboration and demonstrates that they value the team's input.

In essence, embracing authenticity in your personal brand is about integrating who you are into every aspect of your professional life. It's about being clear on your values, consistent in your actions, open about your journey, and willing to be vulnerable when it matters. This is not just a strategy—it's a way of being that builds trust, fosters connection, and ultimately, sets you apart as a leader who is as real as they come.

When Staying True Is Tough

Authenticity can be a double-edged sword for leaders operating in environments that undervalue certain leadership qualities. Traits like empathy, collaboration, or vulnerability—essential for fostering trust and inclusivity—are too often dismissed as "soft" skills rather than strengths. In cultures that reward pushiness over teamwork or label directness as abrasive based on the individual, staying true to one's values can feel isolating and undervalued.[6]

As Herminia Ibarra, The Charles Handy Professor of Organizational Behavior at London Business School, explores in The Authenticity Paradox,[7] authenticity isn't about rigidly adhering to a fixed identity. Instead, it's about embracing a dynamic approach—staying grounded in evolving values while adapting to meet new challenges. Building a personal brand rooted in authenticity doesn't guarantee instant acceptance, particularly in environments misaligned with one's principles. Yet, it empowers leaders to make a lasting impact by forging connections with the right people and opportunities, even if it requires stepping away from settings that don't align.

For example, after a company acquisition, a senior leader might find themselves in a toxic workplace where self-centered behavior and public criticism overshadow inclusivity and collaboration. Their empathetic leadership style, which values trust and growth, could clash with the prevailing culture, making it nearly impossible to achieve the outcomes they envision. Ultimately, they might make the difficult decision to leave, recognizing that their authenticity and values can't thrive in such an environment. This choice reaffirms their commitment to leading with integrity and paves the way for personal and professional growth.

This example underscores Ibarra's key insight: embracing authenticity doesn't mean staying static—it means evolving and making deliberate choices that reflect your principles while adapting to the demands of leadership. Leaders who balance integrity with adaptability can build deeper relationships, cultivate trust, and find opportunities that resonate with their core values.

Expertise

I like to think of expertise the same way a startup would approach building a Unique Value Proposition (UVP) to differentiate itself. I believe that expertise in personal branding emerges from the fusion of core skills, lived experiences, and a unique perspective—all elements that distinguish you and make your brand resonate.

Skills form the bedrock of your expertise, whether they're technical, interpersonal, creative, or analytical. These are the strengths people recognize in you, the abilities that have become your professional signature. Perhaps you're known for your talent in connecting the dots across domains or simplifying complex problems—a quality that sets you apart. For me, my expertise is rooted in building and leading vibrant communities. I've honed skills in public speaking, communication, and leadership. People often say, "Anna has this incredible ability to bring people together and inspire them to take action." Whether leading WomenTech Network or speaking at global conferences, these skills have become my signature in the tech world.

Then there's your real-life, lived experience. This is the path you've taken, with all its ups and downs, valleys, and hills. Your story—the environment you grew up in, the successes you've achieved, the failures you've learned from, and the challenges you've faced—is what adds depth to your expertise and personal brand. When we build products and services, we don't design them for "perfect," "emotionless," and "identical" individuals. Our lived experiences enable us to connect with others on a deeper level—be it customers, team members, or leadership.

Growing up in Ukraine in a middle-class family, I developed resilience and adaptability early on. Later, as an immigrant and working mother navigating life across various countries and cultures, I've faced challenges that strengthened my character and broadened my perspective. These experiences have deepened my understanding and ability to relate to people from diverse backgrounds, and enhanced my expertise as a leader.

And this brings us to your perspective—the unique lens through which you see the world. Literally, there's no one else like you, even if you have a twin. Your worldview is influenced by your background, culture, values, and everything else that makes up your identity. This perspective allows you to connect the dots in ways others might not, offering fresh and impactful insights that truly set you apart.

My path, cultural heritage, and unique experiences have given me a distinct worldview, which drives me to address significant questions, like the underrepresentation of women in tech, and to push for meaningful, lasting change. It's this combination of skills, experiences, and perspective that not only defines my personal brand but also fuels my passion for making a real impact in the industry.

Mira Murati: A Brand Built on AI Innovation and Expertise

Mira Murati's personal brand centers on her expertise in shaping groundbreaking AI technologies like ChatGPT, DALL-E, and GPT-4, combined with her commitment to ethics in AI development. As the CTO at OpenAI, Murati has played a pivotal role not only in driving technical advancements but also in embedding ethical considerations into these innovations. Her brand reflects a unique blend of deep technical expertise, a commitment to responsible AI, and a global perspective informed by her diverse experiences. This combination has positioned her as a leading voice in AI—one who champions both innovation and integrity, striving to create technology that is as ethical as it is transformative.

Murati's personal brand is shaped by her expertise, her unique journey and unwavering commitment to ethical technology. Growing up in Albania during a time of political transition, she developed an intense curiosity and passion for science, inspired by her early love of mathematics. This foundation, combined with her experiences moving to Canada and then to the United States, broadened her perspective, giving her a distinctly global outlook. These experiences have become core elements of her brand: a leader who brings cultural awareness, intellectual rigor, and a dedication to responsible AI to her work.

Visibility

Myth: Your work speaks for itself.
Reality: You need to speak about your work.

Don't get me wrong—I absolutely believe in the power of hard work and its potential to yield rewards. However, as workplaces become more competitive and fast-paced, hard work alone is no longer sufficient. If your work is behind the scenes and your contributions aren't recognized, you're on the fast track to being overlooked, particularly in companies where transparency around promotions and recognition is lacking.

Think about your career as an investor diversifying their portfolio. Just as an investor seeks to maximize returns by spreading investments across various assets, you should aim to maximize your professional impact by ensuring that people across different departments are aware of your contributions and the impactful work you're delivering. This requires a shift in mindset—from focusing solely on doing great work to also ensuring that your work is seen, appreciated, and recognized by the right people within your organization.

Adopting this mindset means being strategic about where and how you share your achievements. Ask yourself critical questions like, "What new ways can I make the biggest impact in the company?" and "Who else should I connect with to expand my influence?"

By identifying key stakeholders—leaders in other departments, influential peers, or potential sponsors—you can engage them through meetings, cross-functional projects, or informal conversations (more on networking in Chapter 4 and on sponsorship in Chapter 5). Building these relationships increases the number of people who are aware of your capabilities, leading to new opportunities and enhanced visibility.

How to Enhance Visibility at Work

Raji Subramanian, former CTO at Opendoor,[8] shared crucial advice for women looking to increase their visibility at work. Her recommendation is to focus on what she calls "vertical results." Subramanian explains, "Women typically tend to go after horizontal results; I would highly encourage women to take on vertical, visible results."

In Subramanian's words, "horizontal results" are broad contributions like improving processes or supporting team initiatives, which, while valuable, may not be as visible or career-advancing as "vertical results"—those directly tied to high-impact, measurable business outcomes that get noticed by leadership.

So how do you focus on "vertical results"? The answer is simple: choose projects that have a direct and measurable impact on the company's bottom line. These are typically the kinds of achievements that not only gain high visibility and recognition but also stay in the minds of decision-makers when it's time to discuss promotions and leadership opportunities. Subramanian stressed that simply doing good work isn't enough; women need to actively communicate their achievements to the right people. "Your achievements need to be visible…. It's about making sure that the right people know the value you're bringing to the table."

To identify and seek projects and opportunities that lead to high-impact results, Subramanian advises seeking out opportunities to contribute to high-level discussions and decision-making processes. This not only enhances your visibility at work but also positions you as a key player in shaping the company's direction. "Are you participating in the strategic aspects of the company? This is key to crossing the bridge from tactical to strategic thinking."

Subramanian also emphasized the importance of actively demonstrating and communicating your technical depth to ensure it's acknowledged. "Being able to get recognition for your technical chops is not always a given…. Your competence and your success have to stand out."

Visibility in High-Stake Meetings

Suman Rao, VP of US Business Technology & Analytics at HelloFresh,[9] highlighted the intentionality of visibility at work: "It's not just about doing the work but projecting yourself as a leader. We [women] often take on more tasks, thinking, 'I'll do it, I'll do it,' without considering if it's moving us forward."

Rao's experience emphasizes the importance of not just delivering results but ensuring that those results are visible to the right people. She adds that "Men, at least from my observations, are very strategic in terms of what they do and how they play the game."

Rao vividly recalls a pivotal moment in her career that changed her approach to self-promotion: "I was in a board meeting, presenting my credentials, and I spoke for about two minutes," she recounts. After the meeting, a mentor, the CFO at the time, pulled her aside and gave her crucial feedback: "You did a great job. But you could have spoken for five minutes about everything that you've done now.'"

This advice was a turning point for Rao. "She [the mentor] pushed me to realize that it's okay to talk about yourself, to brag about yourself. That's the platform where you do it," Rao reflects. This experience highlighted for her the importance of fully leveraging opportunities to showcase her work, especially in high-stakes environments like board meetings.

Managing Your Online Presence

When people want to learn more about you, their first instinct is often to Google your name or check your LinkedIn profile. This initial search shapes their impression of you—your expertise, values, and professional identity. Take a moment to Google yourself. What pops up? Does it reflect the professional you are today and the one you aim to be? If not, don't stress—start with simple but effective steps, like updating your professional profiles to ensure consistency and alignment across platforms.

Optimize Your Professional Profiles   For example, you probably think of LinkedIn as your digital business card and resume. But in fact, it goes beyond listing roles or achievements. Every detail, from your headshot to your headline—and yes, your bio—contributes to your personal brand.

Regularly updating your headline ensures it stays relevant to your current roles and aspirations. A strong headline combines your expertise with personal touches that make it memorable. For instance, my headline includes: *"Founder & Global CEO Women Tech Network, Chief in Tech Summit, Keynote Speaker, DITA Trailblazer Award Winner, Author."* This mix of keywords and roles helps the right people discover me. Some leaders also add personal elements like *"Mother | Mentor | Women in Tech Advocate"* or actionable phrases like *"Open to Board Roles."*

Creating a compelling bio is all about showcasing your leadership qualities, strategic vision, and the impact you've made. Start with a strong opening that grabs attention and clearly defines who you are and the value you bring—something like, "Innovative leader in [industry] with a proven track record of driving transformational growth." Focus on your key achievements by highlighting major accomplishments such as revenue growth, team scaling, innovation, or market expansion, and don't shy away from using specific numbers to quantify your success.

Describe your leadership style and how it positively impacts teams and culture; perhaps you're someone who believes in empowering teams and fostering innovation to build lasting success. Highlight your industry expertise by mentioning any specializations or extensive experience you have, especially if it adds depth to your executive role. Including personal values and passions, like a dedication to sustainability or mentorship, adds a human touch and shows what drives you beyond the office.

For example, if you've held notable roles or titles—like being a former VP of engineering at a known company or serving on an advisory board—be sure to mention them to add credibility. Using industry-relevant keywords throughout your bio can improve your visibility across search-engines, so think about the skills, technologies, and leadership roles that define your experience.

Keep your bio concise and easy to read, aiming for a format that's engaging even on mobile devices. Additionally, it's wise to include a simple disclaimer on your social profiles, such as "My posts are my own and do not reflect the opinions of my current or past employers."

Balancing authority, achievements, and approachability will make your bio both impressive and relatable to potential connections and partners.

Create and Share Valuable Content   Building credibility goes beyond maintaining a polished profile. It's about actively creating and sharing content that reflects your expertise and passions. Share articles, updates, and insights that add value to your network. For example, Reshma Saujani, founder of Girls Who Code, transitioned her personal brand to focus on advocating for working mothers through her "Moms First" initiative. Her online presence now reflects this mission, aligning with her current goals and passions. Similarly, your posts should evolve as your interests and expertise grow. If a topic no longer excites or aligns with you, be bold enough to shift.

High-quality content doesn't have to be overwhelming to produce. Start by sharing thoughtful insights, reposting articles with your perspective, or commenting on trending industry news. Don't forget to use relevant hashtags to expand your reach—hashtags like *#personalbranding* and *#networking* are widely followed, but creating your own unique hashtag tied to your brand can further distinguish you. Also, share podcasts, interviews, or panels where you've participated to showcase your "expert work." These formats not only amplify your voice but also allow people to connect with your story on a deeper level.

For those less comfortable with public speaking or live streams, start with what feels manageable. Perhaps an interview or a written blog is the right starting point. Over time, you can expand to podcasts, video content, or speaking engagements. Growth often requires stepping out of your comfort zone, but intentionality about where you want to grow makes the process more manageable.

As your online presence grows, monitoring your digital footprint ensures it remains a strong reflection of your evolving goals. Setting up Google Alerts for your name or key topics in your field is an easy way to stay informed about how and where your brand is being mentioned. Regular audits help you address outdated content or inaccuracies promptly.

Managing your online presence is an evolving process, and there's no one-size-fits-all approach. Some people excel at crafting their brand independently, while others may choose to delegate certain aspects to professionals. I've tried outsourcing the building of my personal brand—not once, but twice. Each time, it didn't quite work out. Not because the teams weren't skilled, but because I realized something fundamental: I genuinely enjoy writing content, engaging with my network, and experimenting with my style. It's not always easy, and I'm far from perfect, but this hands-on approach aligns with my vision of sustaining and growing an authentic brand.

That said, it's about finding what works for you. Many professionals work with PR or communications teams, either at their companies or externally, to refine their strategy. These teams can provide invaluable insights, help analyze your channels, and even transform your ideas into compelling content. The key is authenticity. Even if someone else helps you craft or post, the words and experiences must still feel like they're yours.

Building a personal brand isn't just about what you can do alone—it's also about leveraging the resources around you. Many companies are supportive of their employees' branding efforts, offering budgets for training, speaking engagements, or professional memberships. If your company provides access to these resources, take advantage of them. Not only can they help you develop a sustainable and standout brand, but a strong personal brand often brings value back to your organization—a win-win situation.

Whether you choose to go the DIY route or bring in external support, remember that building your online presence takes time and experimentation, but with every step, it becomes easier. The more recognized you become, the more selective you can be with opportunities. Ultimately, this process is about aligning your brand with your goals, staying authentic, and creating meaningful, long-term impact.

One of the easiest ways to keep your content flowing is to repurpose what you've already created. If you've written a blog post that resonated with your audience, why not break it down into a series of social media posts? Or if you've presented at a conference, take the key takeaways or snippets from your presentation and turn them into engaging posts. By recycling and adapting your existing content, you can reach new audiences and reinforce your key messages without constantly starting from scratch.

Summarize projects you've worked on by focusing on problem-solving strategies and outcomes, and highlight any innovative approaches or technologies you've used. You can adapt code snippets, project documentation, or user guides into how-to articles or tutorials. If you've participated in panels or interviews, turn those questions and your responses into a Q&A-style article or a series of posts. You could even convert your workshop content into downloadable resources or online courses, extending your reach and impact. Just remember to always check your company's policies to see how much you're allowed to share externally—it's important to stay within those guidelines while building your personal brand.

Staying the Course with Intention

There was a pivotal moment for me when I decided to "get serious" about my content on LinkedIn. I took a hard look at all the posts I had shared over the last year and realized that they were mostly tied to what we were doing at WomenTech Network—whether it was the Global Conference or the Global Awards. While that content was valuable, it focused more on the company brand than on my personal brand. I knew something had to change if I wanted people to learn from my insights and experiences throughout the year, not just from what the organization was doing.

So, I told myself: "Just post it!" I committed to sharing content at least once a week, no matter how busy I was. It wasn't easy—there were times when I was too tired or uninspired—but I stuck with it. Most of my top-performing posts were crafted on weekends when I had the time to research and refine them.

As I continued, I saw the results: increased engagement, new opportunities, and significant growth in my network. One post even went viral after being reshared by a major publication.

To distill the approach that worked for me, use the tips below to make it work for you:

Commit to a Consistent Schedule Decide to post regularly, whether that's once a week, biweekly, or monthly. There are metrics and algorithms and, not like I recommend ignoring them, but when you set "unrealistic expectations" you will be just lagging behind and feeling like you are underperforming. Yes, consistency is key, but consistency should be on your terms, so even if you're busy, aim to stick with this schedule to keep your audience engaged. Literally block time each week or month for creating or brainstorming content and "just do it." Don't wait until you feel inspired.

Make Time for Content Creation Writing posts on LinkedIn or other social networks takes time. Set aside a few hours during quieter times (like weekends or evenings) for research, writing, and refining your posts. This dedicated time allows you to craft thoughtful, high-quality content that resonates with readers.

Focus on Quality Over Quantity Share content that genuinely helps or inspires your audience. Posts that offer clear insights, tips, or stories will attract engagement from industry leaders over time, helping you build credibility.

If you need a break, take it, but stay intentional about reconnecting. When you come back, focus on adding value right away to re-engage your audience. Share a story, lesson, or reflection from your time away to remind your followers why they follow you.

The Power of Recommendations and Testimonials

Unless you're a household name like Ginny Rometty or Sheryl Sandberg, gathering recommendations is invaluable—even if you're not actively seeking a new role. When colleagues, managers, or clients endorse your skills and achievements, their words act as powerful, visible proof of your expertise, adding credibility and reinforcing your brand. While a bio can showcase your strengths, authentic recommendations elevate your impact, as others share how you've helped them succeed. This validation from respected voices makes your brand shine beyond what you could convey alone, building a reputation rooted in real influence and support. To make things easier, when asking for a recommendation, testimonial, or endorsement provide them with a draft highlighting the skills and experiences you wish to be emphasized, and follow up to ensure they complete it.

In many cases, it's all about the right timing to collect your "moments of impact":

- You just spoke at an event and it was a success? Ask for a recommendation.
- You mentored a director who just got that so-desired VP role at a company they've been aiming to join for years? Ask for a recommendation.
- You're looking for a new role and want to build more credibility on your profile? Ask for a recommendation.
- Your client is happy with your work? Ask for a testimonial.

There's also incredible value in giving recommendations to both senior professionals and rising stars. Whenever someone checks their profile, they'll see your recommendation and might also check out your profile.

Alongside offering recommendations, I've found value in giving early praise and testimonials for impactful book authors within my network, such as Alana Karen (*The Adventures of Women in Tech*), Edwige A. Robinson (*Believe It's Possible*), Shelmina Babai Abji (*Show Your Worth*).

The Power of Awards for Your Personal Brand

I remember winning my first-ever professional achievement award. It felt surreal and almost unbelievable. For a moment, I even felt like an imposter, but then I shook off that feeling, remembering all the long hours, sleepless nights, stress, perseverance and hard work. It wasn't a lottery I won by accident. It was because of the impact I made in the tech community when we organized the first-ever virtual Women in Tech Global Conference at the peak of COVID in 2020. My point here? In the long run, that first award gave me the confidence I needed at that time. It contributed greatly to growing my personal brand.

Of course, the more awards you win, the more important it becomes to stay humble. A great rule of thumb is not to let success go to your head. I have another rule: I don't celebrate my successes for longer than 24 hours, and I also don't let myself dwell on my failures for more than 24 hours. It's not always perfectly measured, but as a mindset, it works.

When I talk to women in our community and beyond, they often share how external confirmation—like winning an award—gives them the encouragement they need and makes a difference in their careers. Recognition on a global level helped them get promoted, boosted their confidence to ask for a raise (and they got it), positioned them for higher-level jobs (ones they hadn't dared to apply for), helped secure funding, and got them featured in national and international media outlets, podcasts, and more.

Self-nominating is a great way to reflect on the progress you've made. If you do it regularly, you'll also keep track of your most outstanding achievements with key stats, metrics, and results. It gives you an outside perspective, which is especially helpful if you struggle with imposter syndrome.

Essentially, each award enhances your story, showcasing growth and potential. Thoughtfully leveraged, these achievements can inspire others while building an authentic personal brand and shaping your leadership journey.

As we wrap up this chapter, remember that Personal Brand = (Authenticity + Expertise) $\star$ Visibility—serves as a guide for crafting a brand that truly reflects who you are and what you stand for.

Building a strong personal brand is a deeply *personal* business. When you bring intention, consistency, and a bit of courage into the mix, your brand can open doors, build trust, and create opportunities you never thought possible. Remember that your personal brand is going to evolve as you do. But you know what? The real magic is in the journey itself. Every challenge, every win, every lesson—it's all shaping the leader you're becoming. So, go ahead and embrace it. Let your brand not only show where you are but also the amazing potential of where you're headed.

- **Embrace Authenticity**: Stories are 22 times[10] more memorable than facts alone. This week, share a challenge you've overcome or a lesson learned. How can revealing your true self forge deeper connections?
- **Highlight Your Unique Expertise**: Your unique skills and experiences set you apart. Identify 3–5 core topics you want to be known for and plan to share insights on these regularly. How can you integrate your strengths into your professional persona to stand out?
- **Champion Your Achievements**: Don't let the "hidden gem"[11] syndrome hold you back. Identify 3–5 award opportunities to nominate yourself or ask someone to nominate you. What achievements can you confidently craft into a storyline to enhance your credibility?
- **Expand Your Influence**: Research and identify 5–10 industry publications or media outlets that align with your brand. Find 3–5 conferences, panels, or podcasts where you can speak on your areas of expertise. What platforms can best position you as an industry leader and help you reach your ideal audience?
- **Audit Your Digital Footprint**: What updates—like a video introduction or showcasing passion projects—can you add to reflect your evolving brand?
- **Give and Seek Endorsements**: Reach out to 5–10 mentors, colleagues, or clients for recommendations highlighting your impact. Who can provide a vivid account of your contributions to enhance your personal brand?

4

Expanding and Leveraging Your Professional Network

Networking is the #1 unwritten rule of success—for
work and life.
—Sallie Krawcheck, CEO and Founder of Ellevest[1]

A few years into my career, I was so focused on improving my skills and deepening my expertise that I believed hard work alone would be enough to reach the next level. But as I looked around at the women leaders I admired, I noticed they all had something in common—a strong professional network. They didn't rely solely on what they knew; they relied on who they knew—people who opened doors, offered insights, and shared fresh perspectives when it mattered most.

Research[2] supports this idea, showing that networking significantly amplifies career success. Further, a study called "The Networking Effect"[3] analyzed more than two billion professional connections and found that companies with well-connected employee networks create more valuable and successful innovations, with patents that make a bigger impact in the market.

In this chapter, we'll explore ways to build lasting professional relationships. We'll look at strategies to expand your network beyond your immediate circle and connect with communities that align with your values and ambitions. Building a successful network means finding people who champion you, support your growth, and offer insights that propel you forward. We'll also discuss how to nurture these connections and leverage your network—not only for advice, job search, or introductions (which, when approached thoughtfully, can be highly impactful) but also for collaboration and new opportunities.

Building Your Professional Network

So, how do you build a network that truly supports your growth? It all starts with understanding your "why"—the purpose behind your connections and what you aim to achieve.

When I became a Founder Institute Director, my purpose was to spread awareness about the world's largest accelerator program in the world and to attract founders, mentors, and advisors. Everywhere I went, I networked with this purpose in mind, making sure each interaction was aligned with my mission.

One Chief Product and Technology Officer, shared her belief in purposeful networking over casual connections. "I've never been particularly good at networking for the sake of it. I find it much easier where it's like a panel discussion and someone having a talk, and then there's something specific that you can sort of start to bring about." Her approach is a reminder that networking isn't about collecting contacts but about finding shared interests and challenges to drive meaningful conversations. This kind of focus transforms each interaction into a purposeful, intentional experience that brings real value and depth.

When I first started organizing events for women in tech, my "why" was clear: I wanted to build a community where like-minded women could learn, connect, and grow together. This purpose shaped every conversation I had, turning each interaction into something intentional and meaningful. Knowing your "why" gives you a strong foundation—a guiding sense of direction that helps you connect with people who align with your goals.

Take a moment to think about what you really want—and need—from your network. Are you looking to advance in your field, build a community of supporters, explore new directions, or perhaps, create strategic partnerships that amplify your organization's impact? When you're clear on this, networking transforms: it stops being about collecting business cards or LinkedIn connections and becomes all about cultivating purposeful, impactful relationships.

In a conversation with Devshree Golecha, Head of Enterprise Data & Business Intelligence at Step Up For Students,[4] she emphasized the importance of value-driven networking: "When you start networking from the perspective that there could be a win-win for both parties, I think then it makes more sense."[5] When you approach networking with this mindset it becomes a mutual exchange rather than a one-sided endeavor. A great way to think about this to ask "How can we both grow from this?"

In practice, networking has been about seeking guidance from women who've taken paths I aspired to follow. Their shared insights—whether on leadership, the importance of soft skills, or navigating challenges—have provided invaluable lessons, saving me time and effort while helping me grow both personally and professionally.

Reaching out to senior leaders outside my immediate circles of aspiration has added another dimension to my networking experience. While I initially sought to learn from their expertise, our exchanges often proved mutually beneficial. They gained access to my network, and insight into the unique challenges women in tech face today. Research from *Harvard Business Review* on "Managing Up" supports this, showing that mutual benefit when connecting with senior leaders deepens understanding of diverse workplace challenges, ultimately enriching both perspectives.

Keeping a pulse on tech's fast-turn world is yet another reason I lean into networking; colleagues often introduce me to new tools and strategies, which I, in turn, share with others. The LinkedIn Learning Workplace Learning Report[6] highlights that peer-to-peer networking is a top way for professionals to keep up with evolving industry trends.

But at the heart of it all, my compound "why" is creating a support network—one where we uplift each other, celebrate wins, and grow stronger together. A survey by the American Psychological Association[7] highlights the psychological benefits of social support networks, where such support fosters emotional resilience.

Expand Beyond Your Immediate Circle

We tend to invest heavily in building connections with those closest to us on the organizational chart—our peers, our direct reports, and the colleagues we work with every day. This focus makes sense; these relationships can make or break our immediate success. As leaders we need to innovate, problem-solve, and be creative but how often do we seek out perspectives from those outside our immediate circle?

Don't limit yourself to people you already know. Grace Pérez, former Chief Digital Program Officer, GE HealthCare,[8] shared with me: "Women often tend to network where they feel comfortable, but real growth happens when you step outside that comfort zone. Networking should be about looking toward where you want to go and who you want to become, and that means breaking through barriers and stretching yourself."[9] Engaging in diverse gatherings, as *Harvard Business Review* research suggests, fosters innovation and problem-solving by introducing fresh ideas and perspectives.

Pérez once shared how she met a valuable mentor through a guitar class—networking in non-work environments, she said, "can also be pretty key." Inspired, I joined a local yoga group. Not only did it help me unwind and reduce stress, but I also connected with professionals from various industries who offered unique viewpoints, allowing me to see things from different angles. According to *Stanford Business School*,[10] such casual connections in relaxed settings are often highly impactful, as they allow more genuine, open exchanges that benefit both parties personally and professionally. It's a reminder that meaningful connections can form anywhere, not only in formal, work-related spaces.

When you're constantly in your "professional bubble," it's easy to miss details essential for seeing the big picture or solving a problem in a creative way. For me, exploring industry events outside of my usual field has made a huge difference. At first, stepping into different meetups and conferences felt a bit outside my comfort zone. But at one event focused on education, I connected with someone working in e-learning who shared how they used gamification to engage users. Their insights inspired me to try similar strategies in our WomenTech Network community, which ended up driving exponential growth in our Global Ambassador program. Exposure to different approaches in unrelated fields can offer fresh strategies for overcoming challenges in your own work. Also seeking ideas outside your field exposes you to new perspectives, enhancing your problem-solving and strategic thinking. According to *Harvard Business Review*, this type of cross-industry engagement fuels innovation, as diverse perspectives create pathways to unique solutions and collaborations.

The question we should be asking ourselves isn't, "Who's on my team?" rather, "Who else could I learn from and collaborate with to create lasting impact?"

Participate in Cross-Functional Projects at Work

One of the most impactful ways to expand your professional network right where you are is by engaging in cross-functional projects. Working alongside colleagues from different departments doesn't just broaden your skill set—it can lead to future collaborations and open doors to career growth.

The good news is that networking within your organization doesn't have to be a big, formal effort. In fact, the most meaningful connections often happen in the small moments. Instead of setting aside time to "network," you can simply engage through everyday interactions. For example, becoming involved in company-wide Slack or Teams channels, such as Employee Resource Groups (ERGs) or affinity groups, may provide regular opportunities for interaction without the pressure of a formal setting. Simply sharing articles, tips, or asking questions in these spaces helps keep you visible and engaged with colleagues across teams.

Volunteering for cross-functional initiatives, like knowledge management or process improvements, also positions you as a helpful resource.[11] Offering to help with code reviews, joining a hackathon, or participating in task forces that tackle company-wide challenges enables you to contribute meaningfully while meeting colleagues outside of your immediate team. Even volunteering to facilitate lunch-and-learn sessions, where colleagues from different departments share insights, creates a relaxed and collaborative environment.

An intentional approach strengthens these connections. On cross-functional projects, introduce yourself to team members from other departments early on and set up brief check-ins to build rapport. A simple five-minute follow-up or a quick virtual coffee chat can go a long way in establishing a personal connection and aligning on project goals. Asking questions like, "What part of this project are you most excited about?"

during stand-ups or meetings sparks friendly conversation and builds camaraderie.

When a project is complete, consider sharing the results on your company's communication platform, acknowledging everyone's contributions by name. This fosters goodwill and opens doors to future collaborations. Additionally, you can ask HR or your manager about opportunities to sign up for internal mentorship programs, training seminars, or committees to meet colleagues across departments.

Participating in such activities can make your day-to-day work more engaging, and it allows you to demonstrate leadership, build trust, and establish a support network within your organization. As you create these connections, you're investing in your own career growth and contributing to a stronger, more integrated team culture.

Engage with Online Communities and Forums

Many of the most meaningful connections I've built started online. Engaging with online communities and forums has been an incredible way to connect with industry peers, learn from experts, and stay updated on trends from around the world. Specialized platforms such as Slack communities, Discord servers, or Mighty Networks offer excellent opportunities to dive into discussions and build relationships. Additionally, explore professional networks like LinkedIn Groups or forums focused on specific industries or topics, such as Reddit, Quora, and Glassdoor. Seek out active groups that align with your interests and goals, whether it's machine learning, product management, cybersecurity, or women in tech.

Begin by introducing yourself with a brief note about your experience or what you hope to learn, then start small by sharing an article, asking a question, or posting a tip. Even something simple like, "Has anyone faced challenges with XYZ?" can spark insightful discussions. I've found that engaging with niche communities creates meaningful conversations and often leads to unexpected collaborations.

Stay active in online communities to enhance your visibility and keep you top-of-mind for connections who may have opportunities for you down the line. Margaux Miller, a TEDx Speaker, a skilled networker and frequent stage emcee at the Women in Tech Global Conference, advises engaging with others' posts to maintain an active presence. She suggests adding thoughtful comments rather than simply "liking" content to show genuine engagement. Another tip she offers is to tag people relevant to a discussion: "When you're a connector, it really helps others think highly of you."[12] Consistent online engagement allows you to build credibility and foster strong professional ties across different communities.

Strategically Build Your Network on LinkedIn

"Honestly, I hate LinkedIn," a former C-suite tech exec shared with me once. "Okay, hate might be a strong word. I'm not a fan, but I understand the value of it and that you need it."

Hate it or love it, LinkedIn has more than 1 billion users in 200+ countries, making it the world's largest professional networking platform[13], and if you are not using it to build and grow your network strategically you are missing out on a lot.

I remember when I started my career and discovered LinkedIn. I was desperately trying to get to that 500+ connections mark, despite LinkedIn advising you to connect only with people you know or have met. While this is generally good advice, following it would not have allowed me to get where I am now. With 50,000 followers, I've built a substantial network and am now approaching LinkedIn's limit for connections. Platforms like LinkedIn help network without borders, allowing you to stay in touch with people you meet, work with, or want to work with. You can reach out for advice, offer collaboration opportunities, get your next role, or be discovered by a hiring manager.

When connecting, make it personal. Always mention something specific, like a shared interest or an article they wrote. For example, "Hi [Name], I recently read your article on sustainable energy innovations. I'm deeply invested in green technology myself and would love to connect to share insights." This makes the request more genuine and increases the chance of a meaningful connection.

A personalized follow-up message after connecting with someone new can strengthen your connection. For example, Parna Sarkar-Basu, founder of Brand and Buzz Consulting[14] shared, "Most of my professional opportunities came through my network." She further emphasized, "You can't go silent on platforms like LinkedIn and then suddenly pop up when you need something." Expressing genuine interest in a person's work and mentioning specific topics or insights they've shared in posts can set the foundation for a more authentic professional relationship. For instance, "Hi [Name],

I enjoyed your recent talk/post/article on digital transformation. I'd love to hear more about your thoughts on integrating these practices within [your industry/domain]."

Have you ever noticed how a well-placed comment can spark a conversation? Identify leaders in your industry or those who share insights on topics you're passionate about. Start by leaving thoughtful comments on their posts—this often catches their attention and can naturally lead to a connection.

An example could be "@[Author Name] Your recent post on AI in manufacturing struck a chord. We implemented a similar strategy at [Your Company] and saw a 15% efficiency boost. I'd be interested in connecting to discuss shared insights!" Another example is actively participating in discussions by adding solution-oriented comments like, "Great insights, [Name]! I particularly liked your point about [specific point]. Have you considered [related idea/solution/tool]?"

To showcase expertise and build visibility, share insights on industry trends. Craft posts that highlight your knowledge while encouraging meaningful engagement, and consider tagging relevant connections or influencers to foster dialogue and collaboration. For example, "As we see in the latest trends, AI-driven personalization is shaping customer experiences like never before. Curious to hear thoughts from leaders like @[Influencer Name] and @[Connection]. How are you seeing this impact your strategies?"

Harness the Power of Events

Here's a compelling statistic: 81% of professionals who attend events do so specifically to connect with experts.[15] So, at every tech conference, meetup, or summit, the majority are there with the same goal—to build meaningful connections, just like you.

Start by finding events that align with your career goals. Think about it: Who do you want to learn from? Who's doing the work that excites you? Once you're there, don't just attend—network! Before the event reach out to colleagues, peers and speakers who'll be there, set up a coffee chat, and follow up. These small, intentional steps can lead to meaningful insights and relationships that make a real difference in your work and career trajectory.

If your company sponsors or hosts events, check with HR, marketing, or relevant departments to find out who's attending or organizing. Expressing interest and offering to help demonstrates initiative and shows that you're invested in engaging with the community. As a bonus, volunteering at events (like assisting with setup, introducing speakers, or handling social media) can also position you as a familiar face among industry leaders and attendees.

When attending events, focus on engaging in meaningful conversations rather than just collecting contacts. Networking is not a numbers game; it's about quality, not quantity. Start conversations by asking open-ended questions, such as "What inspired you to attend this event?" or "What's been your biggest takeaway from the session so far?" These questions encourage deeper dialogue and help uncover shared interests. Additionally, instead of the usual, "What do you do?" try asking, "What do you enjoy most about what you do at XYZ company?" or "How did you get started in that field?" These subtle shifts encourage people to share their passions and personal journeys, making the conversation more engaging and memorable.

After an event, following up is essential for building lasting connections. Aim to send a quick, personalized thank-you note within a few days—ideally about three, as research[16] shows this timing boosts reply rates by 31% when you reference specific details from your conversation. Try something like, "Hi [Name], it was fantastic meeting you at [Event]! I really enjoyed our chat about [Topic] and would love to keep in touch to explore ways we can collaborate." This thoughtful follow-up reinforces your connection and leaves the door open for future opportunities.

For virtual events, engage actively by participating in Q&A sessions or sharing insights in the chat. This kind of involvement helps build connections and can lead to meaningful conversations. Afterward, consider sharing a summary of what you learned on LinkedIn, mentioning speakers or key contributors. This reinforces learning and keeps the conversation going within your network.

Volunteer or Participate in Industry Organizations

Getting involved in industry organizations is a meaningful way to grow your network while building expertise and credibility. By actively participating in professional groups, you can contribute your skills, learn from peers, and connect with leaders who share your interests.[17]

Becoming a part of that align with your career goals or values, such as Women in Product, Women in AI, or industry-specific associations, provides access to events, resources, and mentorship opportunities that may not be available elsewhere. Volunteering your skills in committees, event planning, or mentoring programs showcases your commitment to the field and can position you as a leader within the community.

Taking on leadership roles within these organizations can significantly raise your profile and help you make a lasting impact. As a member of a board or a committee, you can shape events, set initiatives, and collaborate closely with other members. For instance, organizing workshops or conferences gives you the chance to connect with speakers and sponsors, creating opportunities to establish deeper relationships with industry leaders.

My journey with WomenTech Network began because I couldn't find a community where women in tech could connect and feel a sense of belonging. Asking myself, "Where are all the women in tech?" led me to create the space I wanted to see. While organizations like Women Who Code and Girls in Tech inspired me, I saw gaps that WomenTech Network could fill. Over time, it grew from a small group to a global community. I heard from so many chiefs in tech that they were the only woman on their leadership team, eventually leading to the creation of the Chief in Tech Summit and the Executive Women in Tech (EWIT) network.

The need for women's networks is not new. In the mid-1800s, Ada Lovelace worked on the first algorithm for Charles Babbage's Analytical Engine,[18] pioneering what would become modern computing. Yet, her contributions went largely unrecognized during her lifetime. Decades later, as women started gaining a foothold in male-dominated fields, the first professional networks for women emerged to address the visibility gap and foster mutual support. Early organizations like the Society of Women Engineers (SWE) founded in 1950[19] and later the Anita Borg Institute for Women and Technology (AnitaB.org) laid the foundation for today's communities like WomenTech Network, providing spaces for mentorship, resources, and advocacy.

If you don't have access to like-minded communities nearby, why not start one? Launching a local chapter of an organization or creating a new initiative is a great way to bring together professionals with similar goals and put yourself on the map as a community leader. If you're passionate about a cause, leading an effort like this can help you make an impact, grow your network, and inspire others to join you along the way.

These professional groups also serve as safe spaces where you're no longer the "only one in the room," allowing you to connect with others who understand the unique challenges you may face. Sharing experiences, celebrating successes, and supporting each other within these communities create a sense of belonging that strengthens everyone involved.

Five Effective Networking Tips

Networking is often described as one of the most effective tools for professional growth, yet many of us approach it with hesitation. Why? Because the way we think about networking is often wrong. Awkward introductions, shallow small talk, and a focus on what we can get instead of what we can give—it's no wonder networking feels forced and uncomfortable. But when we reframe networking as an opportunity to connect, to share, and to build meaningful relationships, everything changes.

1. Make a Memorable Impression

Networking often begins with a simple introduction, but the impact of that moment can shape how others perceive you moving forward. It's your chance to stand out, yet I've seen remarkable women with incredible accomplishments hesitate, rushing through their introductions or downplaying their achievements with modest phrases. I know the feeling all too well—imposter syndrome has crept in more times than I care to admit, especially in rooms filled with people who seem more seasoned, or higher ranking. But here's what I've learned: if I'm in the room, it's not by accident—I've earned my place.

I know that networking can sometimes feel "salesy or transactional" but owning your introduction isn't about bragging; it's about letting others see your value and understand the impact of your work. So please allow yourself to be your biggest advocate, and if necessary, give yourself a pep talk to take the time and space—both literally and figuratively—to introduce yourself fully.

A well-crafted introduction sets the stage for meaningful connections and ensures your presence is felt. Normally, when introducing myself, I start with my name and make it memorable by repeating it naturally: "Hi, my name is Anna. Anna Radulovski." This simple habit helps people remember me, especially in crowded spaces where names can easily blur together. But a strong introduction doesn't stop there—it's also about clearly articulating what you do and why it matters. For example, I'd say,

"I am running WomenTech Network, a global community of 150,000 members of women in tech and allies from 179 countries." This pairing of a memorable delivery with a clear statement of value ensures that your introduction leaves a lasting impact.

At a public speaking workshop, I learned the "you know when" technique—a powerful way to explain your work without sounding like a sales pitch. For instance: "You know when companies struggle to attract and retain diverse talent? I organize events and build programs that help organizations overcome that, creating thriving, inclusive workplaces." This approach frames your work around a relatable challenge, making it both engaging and easy to remember. The beauty of this technique is that you can adapt your pitch to your audience, making it easier for them to understand your work and its impact.

Your physical presence matters, too. Maintain open body language—stand tall, make eye contact, and use natural gestures to command attention. Avoid shrinking into your chair or looking away during conversations, as these actions can unintentionally diminish your presence.

Whether it's during a one-on-one conversation, a meeting, a networking event or a conference, taking up space shows that you respect yourself and your place in the room.

2. Remember Names with Intention

Building strong connections begins with a genuine effort to remember people's names—and being intentional and humble enough to ask if you didn't catch it. This isn't just about attentiveness; it's an act of humility and respect.

Making a genuine effort demonstrates a commitment to valuing each person in the room. If I miss a name, I might say, "I'm sorry, I didn't catch your name earlier—could you share it with me again?" or, "I'd love to get your name right—could you guide me on the pronunciation?" Small gestures like these demonstrate our willingness to go beyond our comfort zone, creating a culture of recognition and respect that helps others feel seen and appreciated.

In group settings, using each person's name when addressing them— "Sarah, I think you mentioned…" or "John, I loved your insight on…"— shows attentiveness and reinforces each name in memory. When people introduce themselves, I often repeat their names at least three times naturally during our conversation: "It's nice to meet you, Jessica…. So Jessica, what brings you here today?" and ending with, "Great chatting with you, Jessica." This repetition helps make the name stick without feeling forced.

Following up with a personal note can reinforce names after a large event. Jotting down a name alongside a detail—like "Lily, project manager, loves Italy"—allows me to send personalized follow-ups that show I truly listened. "Lily, it was so nice chatting at the event! Hope your plans for Italy are coming together!"

3. Flip the Script: From "What Can I Get?" to "How Can I Help?"

A turning point in networking for me was this: shifting my focus from "What can I get?" to "How can I help?" It's a mindset I "borrowed" from some of the power connectors and leaders in my own network—people who were generous with their time, resources, contacts, and insights, often with no expectation of anything in return. Sure, it's tempting to think, "How can this person help me?" But the moment you start with, "How can I support you?" everything shifts. That simple question brings immediate value to the conversation, turning what could be a cold transaction into a real connection. So, next time when you are at a networking event, try asking, "What's a challenge you're currently working on solving?" Such questions spark meaningful conversations and open the door for you to offer insights, resources, or connections.

Part of this mindset shift also involves asking for advice instead of favors. This was a game-changing tip I picked up while working with founders and investors. I learned that people are much more receptive to sharing advice than fulfilling direct requests. For instance, instead of asking an investor outright for funding, I'd say, "If you were in my shoes, how would you approach raising Series A?" People love giving advice—it feels collaborative rather than transactional, and it never feels like a favor.

This approach works in any setting. Instead of asking, "Can you help me get a job at your company?" try saying, "I admire your career path and would love to learn from your experiences. Could you share some advice on positioning myself for roles at companies like yours?" Asking for guidance creates a more genuine and comfortable dynamic, often leading to stronger, longer-lasting relationships.

When we approach networking with a transactional mindset, focusing on "What can this person do for me?" the connection tends to feel shallow.

Sure, you might get a favor here or an introduction there, but without a deeper foundation, these connections often fizzle out. People can sense when they're seen as a resource rather than as a person, when they are seen as a title and "an opportunity" to sell to. In fact, it can get extreme at conferences and summits when many people try to find "creative ways" to sell to senior leaders. I can't forget one story an executive shared with me when someone at a conference followed them all the way to the restroom to make a sales pitch. That approach crosses a line—it's not persistent; it's intrusive. When ego drives networking, it turns into a hard sell, focused solely on personal gain rather than mutual respect. Real networking requires us to leave ego at the door.

Then there's the habit of overlooking people who don't seem "useful" at first glance—perhaps they're in a different industry or hold a junior position. But remember the "six degrees of separation"[20] rule: everyone is only a few connections away from someone who could make a difference in your journey. Often, it's the least expected connections that introduce fresh perspectives or open doors we never anticipated.

4. Be Consistent and Strategic

Consistency means making networking a regular priority—not just something you turn to when you're job hunting or need a favor. It's easy to think that because things are going well, networking isn't necessary, or worse, that you're simply too busy for it. Busy with work, deadlines, family, commitments, and all the demands that fill our days. Networking can feel like just one more thing on an already endless list! Tiring. Optional. But when networking slips off the radar, so do the doors it can open—opportunities for mentorship, promotion, sponsorship, or collaboration. So, not networking can mean missing out, even make you invisible, especially at times when being seen is essential.

I make it a point to dedicate at least one hour each week to networking, but during high seasons—when events and opportunities are at their peak—I often find myself spending two to five hours. Set up a routine that works for you. It doesn't have to be a big commitment. Maybe it's inviting someone new to lunch, grabbing coffee once a week, or connecting over a virtual chat. By regularly connecting with fresh faces, you're expanding your network in a meaningful way that keeps you visible, engaged, and open to opportunities that could otherwise pass you by. Of course, you can use these regular networking times to reconnect with existing contacts as well—particularly leaders or peers who are doing something new, exciting, or impactful. Regular touchpoints ensure that your network remains dynamic and supportive, ready to offer value when you need it most.

5. Take Initiative: Invite Yourself to Opportunities

Effective networking also means taking initiative—including inviting yourself to the table instead of waiting for an invitation. Some of the biggest opportunities I've had came from putting myself in rooms I wanted to be in. I didn't wait to be invited. Instead, I reached out to the organizers, shared my accomplishments (like building one of the largest communities for women in tech or my expertise on a certain topic), and highlighted how my participation could add value to their event. That proactive step opened doors I wouldn't have accessed otherwise. So, my point here is not to hold back from creating your own opportunities; whether it's asking to to participate in a high-level meeting, volunteering for a new project, or reaching out to be included in an event. And no, it isn't about being pushy; it's about confidently advocating for yourself and the impact you're ready to make.

I believe no one is inherently bad at networking (even a very introverted introvert); once you have a clear purpose and know your strengths, you can leverage them to build meaningful connections. Everyone has a unique strength in networking, and yours doesn't have to mirror mine. My superpower is a photographic memory that helps me remember faces and names. At conferences, I often recognize people and recall specific details about them, saying, "I think I know you. You were a speaker at one of our past editions of the Women in Tech Global Conference—you're from New York." This ability allows me to build stronger connections by making others feel seen and remembered. Think about what your superpower is. Are you a great listener who makes people feel heard? Are you a natural storyteller who can captivate others' attention and make even complex ideas relatable and memorable? Recognize your unique strength and use it to your advantage in networking.

Networking at the Executive Level

As we progress in our careers, the way we approach networking evolves. For those at mid-career levels, networking may still focus on career advancement, building visibility, and developing supportive mentorship relationships. But as professionals reach senior roles, networking becomes about more than just individual success—it shifts to influencing industry trends, driving organizational impact, and building a legacy.

Executives have a distinct set of challenges. With limited time and high demands, they must become intentional and strategic, engaging in opportunities that align closely with their goals. At this level, networking is about creating fewer but deeper connections that align with broader organizational and industry goals. Rather than attending every event or speaking at every panel, executives carefully select engagements that foster strategic relationships and industry influence, prioritizing quality over quantity in their networking efforts.

Consider the time constraints most executives face. Many turn to exclusive summits, executive dinners[21], and high-impact industry conferences to connect with like-minded peers who understand the unique challenges of senior leadership. These spaces allow them to collaborate on shared challenges, learn about innovative strategies, and sometimes spark collaborations that shape their fields.

Yet, there's an added complexity at the executive level: maintaining confidentiality and balancing exposure. In conversations with peers, executives need to share insights without overstepping boundaries or revealing sensitive information. Setting these boundaries skillfully is essential, allowing them to foster trust and build mutual respect. Relationships that begin here are often built on a foundation of shared values and confidentiality, creating trusted allies in high places.

Networking at this level also means looking beyond the immediate field. To stay innovative, executives often engage with leaders outside their own industries through cross-industry groups or innovation hubs. This diversity of perspectives can reveal fresh solutions to challenges within their own sectors. I've seen firsthand how joining cross-functional councils and collaborating with peers from different sectors can reinvigorate one's approach, introducing new ideas that fuel progress on a broader scale.

For executives, then, networking becomes less about career progression and more about creating a sustainable, positive influence within their industries. When approached with authenticity and respect, these relationships become part of a legacy that outlasts any single role.

In the next section, we'll explore how to strategically leverage the network you've built—turning authentic connections into pathways for mutual success.

Nurturing and Leveraging Your Network

Building a network is just the first step; effectively nurturing and leveraging it is where you unlock its true potential.

For a long time, I was all about building, building, and building. I attended countless events, collected business cards, connected with thousands of professionals on LinkedIn, and even gained access to top-level executives across the globe. But then I realized that despite having this vast network, many of those connections were starting to fade. Some of the relationships felt superficial, and I wasn't fully engaging with the people I had worked so hard to connect with.

That's when I realized that nurturing your network is essential. It's about transforming those connections from a list of names into a community of allies. It's not just about who you know; it's about how well you know them and how you support each other.

One of the most challenging aspects of leveraging your network is knowing how to ask for help without feeling like you're imposing. Early in my career, I hesitated to reach out to people, fearing I'd come across as needy or opportunistic. But I learned that most people are willing—even happy—to assist if approached respectfully and thoughtfully. It's all about be specific and concise when reaching out. Rather than a vague ask, pinpoint exactly how someone can help. Instead of messages like, "Do you know anyone hiring?", try, "I noticed your company is expanding in data science. If possible, I'd appreciate an introduction to the hiring manager to explore leadership opportunities." This approach saves time and makes it easier for them to assist. The goal is to turn "Do you know anyone who…?" into a powerful, targeted question by clarifying the type of person or role you're interested in connecting with as an example.

Don't hesitate to ask super-connectors in your network for introductions. These individuals seem to know everyone in the industry and are often more than willing to connect you with others. If you've identified someone you'd like to meet, reach out to a super-connector you know and politely request an introduction.

For example, you might say: "I noticed you're connected with [Person]. I'd love to meet them to discuss [specific topic or interest] because [briefly explain the value or insights you believe you can bring to the conversation]. Would you be willing to introduce us?"

To make the introduction process fast and easy, you can also include a short message for the super-connector to use when making the introduction. Here's a simple template:

Hi [Person],

I hope you're doing well. I'd like to introduce you to [Your Name], who is [a brief description of your role or expertise]. [Your Name] is interested in connecting with you to discuss [specific topic] and believes there could be valuable insights to share on [related topic or mutual interest]. I'll let you both take it from here!

Best,

[Super-connector's Name]

Balancing requests with respect for others' time is key. Before reaching out, ask yourself: Can I find this on my own? If a quick Google search could provide the answer, consider holding off. Also, be mindful of requests for insights or information that professionals might usually charge for. Keep your message professional, grateful, and concise. Most people appreciate clear, focused messages that show you respect their time and expertise.

Don't take it personally if you don't receive a response right away—or even at all. The more senior or influential the person is, the more gatekeepers and competing priorities stand between them and your message. They usually might not respond, not because they don't want to help; they're probably just swamped. Give it a couple of polite follow-ups, twice max, and then let it go so you don't come off as too pushy. The reasons someone does not respond can range from switching jobs, dealing with a personal event (like a wedding, maternity leave, or illness), managing a family crisis, or facing a work emergency. In other words, life happens, and it's rarely personal. If one connection isn't available, reach out to someone else who might be able to help at that moment. Your network is there for you to tap into different perspectives and resources, so keep exploring options.

Maintaining consistent and thoughtful communication is key to nurturing your network. One effective way to do this is by referencing something specific from your interactions to show that you were genuinely engaged. If someone recommended a book, for instance, you might reach out and say, "I wanted to thank you for suggesting the book on leadership strategies—it's been tremendously helpful." This approach applies to any helpful resource they might have shared, whether it's a tool, a report, or a new strategy.

Regular check-ins are also important. It doesn't have to be frequent or time-consuming—a quick message to share an interesting article (make sure it is actual and relevant), congratulate them on a recent achievement, or simply ask how they're doing can keep the connection alive. When a former colleague was featured in an industry publication, I sent a note saying, "Congratulations on your feature! Your insights on cybersecurity trends were spot-on." These little touchpoints show that you're thinking of them and value the relationship.

I make it a habit to thank people who have helped me, whether it's through a heartfelt email, a handwritten note, or by thoughtfully connecting them with relevant opportunities. I remember when a colleague went out of their way to assist me with a complex project. Afterward, I sent them a personalized thank-you card expressing how their support made a significant difference. Not only did this make them feel appreciated, but it also reinforced our professional bond.

Public recognition can also be incredibly meaningful. If someone has provided valuable insights or assistance, acknowledging them on LinkedIn can boost their visibility and show your appreciation. For example, I might post, "I want to give a shout-out to Maria for her incredible advice on project management tools. Her expertise has streamlined our processes significantly!" By publicly acknowledging their contributions, you not only express gratitude but also help them gain recognition within your shared professional community.

By engaging thoughtfully, expressing genuine gratitude, and acknowledging others' contributions, you transform your network from a list of contacts into a community of allies. These relationships become mutually supportive, enriching both your professional journey and that of those around you.

Building a successful career isn't a solo journey; it's one supported by the collective strength of your network. Sure, overcoming challenges independently is admirable, the truth is that no one really gets to the top alone.

Networking is essential. It's the people who bet on you, those who mention your name in the right rooms, the mentors who guide you, the managers who hired you and the colleagues who share their insights that shape your career. If you've ever wondered, "How the heck does she do that?" It's because she's built a strong, supportive network along the way.

I'm an optimist. I believe there are always people out there who genuinely want to help you succeed. Sometimes, all it takes is being willing to reach out and let them in. Because in the end, it's those connections—the ones you dared to make—that light the way forward.

- **Step Outside Your Comfort Zone**: Up to 85%[22] of jobs are filled through networking, often through contacts beyond the immediate circle. What new communities or industries can you explore to diversify your network?
- **Don't Take Silence Personally**: Not every outreach gets a response, and that's okay. People are busy, and priorities shift—it's part of the process. Could your timing or approach improve your chances? Who in your network could help bridge the connection?
- **Practice Active Listening**: Listening attentively often leads to deeper connections than speaking does. Are you fully engaging with others, or simply waiting for your turn to talk?
- **Offer Before You Ask**: Providing value first builds stronger and more authentic professional relationships. In what ways can you assist someone in your network today without expecting anything in return?
- **Consistency Is Key**: Regular networking leads to significantly more opportunities than sporadic efforts.
  How can you make networking a consistent part of your weekly routine?

5

Mentorship, Sponsorship, and Allyship

Careers are not built in isolation—they're shaped by relationships, opportunities, and the people who believe in you.

—Anna Radulovski

This guiding principle has shaped my own journey and the careers of countless women I've had the privilege of supporting through the Women-Tech Network. It's a reminder that no matter how talented or driven we are, success is often a team effort—one built on the support and advocacy of mentors, sponsors, and allies.

In this chapter, I'll share insights from my experiences and conversations with leaders across the tech world to explore the profound impact of these relationships. We'll examine the unique roles that mentors, sponsors, and allies play in shaping your career, and why understanding the differences between them is essential.

While reflecting on these critical relationships, I came across a podcast episode that stuck with me. Carla Harris—a Wall Street veteran, TED speaker, and a best-selling author interviewed by Adam Grant on his *ReThinking* podcast.[1] What Harris said resonated with me, and I think it's something we all need to keep in mind as we navigate our careers. She made this clear distinction that's worth remembering.

"The mentor is the person you tell the good, the bad, and the ugly to. This is the person that you can share the intimate details of your career with: your fears, your concerns, your mistakes, your triumphs," Harris explained.

Essentially, a mentor is someone who knows the full, unfiltered story of your journey—warts and all. Mentors are not just there for the celebrations; they're there when things go sideways too. And let me tell you, having someone like that in your corner makes all the difference.

In contrast, Harris highlights a crucial point about sponsors that we should all take to heart. She says, "The sponsor is the person who's carrying your paper. You want them focused on the good, the good, and the good."

This distinction is vital. Sponsors aren't the ones you turn to for advice or emotional support. They're your champions—the ones who advocate for you during critical moments, such as promotions, high-stakes projects, or new opportunities. Sponsors focus on your strengths and achievements, ensuring that your work gets the recognition it deserves.

Both mentors and sponsors are vital to career success, but they serve distinct purposes. In the sections ahead, we'll explore how to cultivate these relationships, why you need both, and how to ensure you're making the most of their unique roles in your professional journey.

Building Strong Mentorship Relationships with MOSAIC

Women with mentors are five times more likely to get promoted. Research from Gartner[2] and other sources consistently shows that having a mentor can significantly boost your career trajectory. This means that building a diverse network of mentors—people from different levels, departments, industries, and backgrounds—can be just as powerful, if not more so, than relying on a single senior mentor. A broad support system can offer guidance, challenge your thinking, and help you navigate your career from multiple angles.

To illustrate the multifaceted role mentorship plays in leadership, I developed the MOSAIC framework, where each letter represents a distinct type of mentor, contributing uniquely to your growth and overall success:

- **M**otivators lift you up when the going gets tough.
- **O**peners unlock doors to new opportunities.
- **S**trategists help you plan your next career move.
- **A**dvocates amplify your work and voice.
- **I**nspirers push you to dream bigger.
- **C**hallengers hold you accountable for achieving your best.

If you're reading this book, chances are you already have a mentor or have had a few along the way. I've heard countless stories from the Women-Tech Network community and interviews with executives, and there's a common thread: mentors—both male and female—have played a huge role in their success. And it doesn't always have to be a senior leader.

In fact, Siri Chilazi, Senior Researcher, Women and Public Policy Program at Harvard Kennedy School,[3] emphasizes that "mentorship programs shouldn't just be about pairing up with someone senior in your department. It's about creating meaningful diverse relationships that can provide different perspectives and support your career in various ways."

Now, let's take a closer look at how each role in the MOSAIC framework comes to life, starting with the Motivators. Have you ever found yourself on the verge of giving up, and a colleague stepped in with just the right words of encouragement? That's your Motivator, the mentor who lifts you up when the going gets tough. They may not always have an official "mentor" title, but their encouragement is invaluable. Take Manju Abraham, former Vice President of Engineering at Hewlett Packard Enterprise.[4] Abraham has been a guiding light for many young engineers, but what's interesting is that she didn't have the formal mentors we often hear about. Instead, she built meaningful connections that have stayed with her throughout her career. She told me, "These relationships were vital. They quietly reminded me of my strengths when I needed it most."

Then there's the Openers. These are the mentors who introduce you to new people, ideas, and opportunities—like a key that unlocks doors you didn't even know were there. Padmaja Dasari, CIO at Nextdoor,[5] shared her approach to this. She believes in building authentic relationships first, before asking someone to be a mentor. "It's about forming a genuine connection first," Dasari emphasized. This thoughtful strategy not only strengthens the mentoring relationship but also ensures that the guidance is rooted in mutual respect and understanding.

Next up is the Strategists—those mentors who help you chart your career path with clarity and foresight. These are the people you go to with specific questions when you need guidance on your next steps. Swetha Kolli, Regional Leader, Product Delivery and Customer Experience at Palo Alto Networks,[6] has mastered the art of navigating her career with the support of mentors both inside and outside her company. She would approach her mentors with focused questions and ask, "How can I effectively navigate this challenge?" or "What do I do in these situations?" Whether it was dealing with workplace dynamics, preparing for a critical presentation, or exploring potential career moves, her questions were always targeted and purposeful. That's exactly what a Strategist does—they help you plan your moves, anticipate potential obstacles, and think several steps ahead.

A represents the Advocates. These are the mentors who don't just guide you—they go to bat for you. They're the ones who make sure your hard work gets the recognition it deserves. Suman Rao, Vice President, US Business Technology & Analytics at HelloFresh,[7] shared with me, "Most mentors focus on guiding you, but you need a champion at a higher level who can speak for you." It's such an important distinction. While mentors offer support, advocates are the ones who champion you, push you forward, making sure your name gets heard in the right places, even beyond your current workplace.

And then we have the Inspirers. These are the mentors who push you to think bigger, dream bolder, and reach higher. They're the visionaries who help you see possibilities that you might not even realize are there. Inspirers are all about expanding your horizons and giving you the confidence to go after those big, audacious goals. They make you believe in yourself, showing you that not only can you survive, but you can thrive and shine.

Finally, the Challengers—the mentors who won't let you settle for anything less than your best. Unlike the Inspirers, who get you excited about the future, Challengers focus on what you're doing right now. They call you out when you're playing it safe and push you to take action. Challengers aren't here to make you comfortable; they're here to ensure you're growing. It's not always easy to have a Challenger in your corner, but their influence can be transformative. By pushing you to think differently, act boldly, and strive for more, they help you achieve levels of success you might not have thought possible.

Each type of mentor plays a unique and crucial role in your journey. Together, they form a mosaic—a diverse, dynamic support system that helps you grow, achieve, and lead with impact. As you progress in your career, it's important to assemble your own MOSAIC, understanding that every mentor, every piece of advice, and every bit of support shapes the leader you're becoming.

It's important to note that you won't need the same amount of time or input from each mentor type. You might spend more time with Motivators, who offer continuous encouragement to keep you focused and energized. Openers, on the other hand, may appear periodically, introducing new opportunities when you're ready to take the next step. In contrast, Challengers might engage with you just once or twice a year to critically evaluate your progress, identify areas where you may be holding back, and push you to take bold actions that stretch you beyond your comfort zone.

When you have multiple mentors—and you should seek advice from different ones—you'll often receive diverse perspectives, and sometimes even contradictory advice. It's important to weigh your options carefully and trust yourself to make the final decision.

You might be disappointed if you look for one mentor to fit all these roles. It's extremely rare to have all these types of mentors at once, so you'll need different people for different parts of your journey. That's how you build a strong, resilient support system that can see you through the highs and lows of your career. Keep your eyes open, be deliberate about the relationships you want to build, and remember that mentorship is a two-way street. The more you give back, the more you—and those around you—will thrive.

The Value of Mentorship

Elaine Montilla, CTO at Pearson and Founder of 5xminority,[8] shared her journey and the pivotal role mentors played in her career. Early on, she faced challenges such as self-doubt and a lack of representation. However, her determination to succeed led her to seek out mentors who believed in her potential and provided invaluable support.

Montilla's mentors embodied various roles within the MOSAIC framework. For example, her senior executive mentor acted as a Motivator, providing both career guidance and emotional support. This mentor helped her navigate the complexities of the tech industry, offering encouragement during difficult times and reinforcing her confidence. She reflected, "Learning to be comfortable being uncomfortable is what helped me move up the ladder."

During a pivotal moment in her career, another mentor stepped in as a Challenger, urging her to confront her fears and push her boundaries with the advice, "Fear is there, but do it anyway." This guidance motivated her to take bold actions, overcome self-doubt, and embrace new challenges.

Reflecting on her growth, Montilla shared, "I realized that even though I was one person, I too could help others." This realization led her to start mentoring young women and men in tech, paying forward the support she received. Her story underscores the collective effort of mentorship—how each role contributes to a career journey, enabling individuals to reach new heights and empowering them to lift others along the way.

The Advice That Sticks

One of the most powerful aspects of mentorship is the lasting impact of a few well-timed words of wisdom. During my conversation with Linda Yao, COO and Head of Strategy, Solutions and Services Group, Lenovo,[9] she shared something that really resonated with me. We were discussing the influence of mentorship, and she told me about a piece of advice she received early in her career that has guided her ever since. Her mentor told her, "Be bright, be brief, and then be gone."

She explained how this advice taught her to always bring something valuable to the table—something insightful and worth everyone's time. "I followed that advice in all the most important conversations," she said, emphasizing how it's helped her stay focused and respectful of others' time, especially in high-stakes meetings or presentations. The idea was to make your point clearly, don't drag it out, and then know when to step back. "And so far, I think it has served me well," she added. This approach also helped Yao build a reputation for being efficient and respectful of others' time, which is crucial in leadership roles.

As a C-level leader, I can confirm that the more specific and concise your request, the more likely you are to get a response. For me, long, overly formal emails aren't just impractical—they often feel impolite in regard to one's time. My favorite ChatGPT prompt is "shorten, shorten, shorten!" When coaching a team member on reaching out to a senior executive, I advised her to focus on key details with a clear call to action. She worried it might seem rude, but I reassured her: "Absolutely not. Concise, clear and purposeful communication earns respect." Being mindful of a leader's time is always more effective than over-complicating your message.

Similarly, Sandy Carter, COO at Unstoppable Domains,[10] reflected on the powerful guidance she received from her mentor, which echoed Maya Angelou's famous words: "I've learned that people will forget what you said, people will forget what you did, but people will never forget how you made them feel."[11] Carter shared, "I try to always think about that." This principle has guided her throughout her career, helping her prioritize meaningful interactions and build lasting relationships.

Approaching Mentors Effectively

One of the key insights I've gathered from speaking with C-level executives is the importance of being specific in your requests.

Grace Pérez, former Chief Digital Program Officer at GE HealthCare,[12] shared some valuable advice on engaging a mentor effectively. She highlighted the need to actively seek out mentors and to be clear in your approach. "Sometimes I was successful, sometimes I wasn't. I would actually reach out to people and ask, 'Could I meet with you for 15 minutes once a month?' It's very hard to get more than that with a very busy senior leader. If they're C-suite, 10 minutes is all you need. Come prepared, come extremely organized, and have questions...no more than two questions that really are going to help you succeed," she said.

Janet Robertson, Global CIO, RS Group,[13] also offered specific advice on how to approach a mentor, stressing the importance of clarity and focus when making a request. "I've had a lot of people ask, 'Can you mentor me?' And I say, 'Well, I don't have a lot of regular time, but if you have specific things you want help with, I'm happy to assist.' The best approach I've seen is when someone says, 'I saw this, and something you said resonated with me,' or 'I watched your presentation on this topic,' or 'There's something specific I'd like to learn from you,'" Robertson shared.

Unless you're part of a formal mentoring program where you're the mentee and the other person is designated as the mentor, the "Will you be my mentor?" approach usually doesn't work. You need to be specific. I remember reaching out to a C-level executive, a founder, for advice on transitioning back to work after giving birth. I was in the early stage of my pregnancy, around the beginning of my second trimester, but I was already thinking of how to make it work after becoming a mom. She was incredibly approachable yet super busy. My request wasn't typical, but I was specific, so she said, "Yes, let's grab coffee." We had a meaningful chat where she shared invaluable advice. She emphasized, "Set clear expectations with your team," and, "Prioritize tasks to protect your energy." Her insights on boundary-setting were pivotal, and her final encouragement: "We need more women like us." It gave me confidence that I could balance motherhood while continuing the work I love. I didn't call her my mentor, but in that moment, she was exactly that—a mentor and a role model for me.

Being a Mentor

In my conversations with executives for this book, I asked what mentorship means to them. Their responses reflected diverse yet recurring themes: mentorship is both a responsibility and an opportunity to guide others while continuing to grow personally. Many saw it as a way to pay forward the support they once received, shaping future leaders and creating lasting impact.

Cindy Taibi, former CIO of *The New York Times*,[14] shared how her own mentors helped her navigate challenging times. "I've had incredible mentors who guided me through tough moments, and now I make it a point to mentor others. It's about giving back and helping others navigate their paths."

For her, mentorship is not just a professional duty but an act of gratitude and leadership.

Dana DiFerdinando, former Chief Data Officer at GE HealthCare,[15] also felt a strong desire to give back, which led her to embrace mentorship and advisory roles. "I wanted to give back, and being a mentor allows me to do that. It's about making sure that the experiences I've gained can help others on their path," DiFerdinando explained. This commitment to mentoring has allowed her to continue making a positive impact beyond her corporate roles.

Rebecca Gasser, Partner and Global Chief Information Officer, FGS Global,[16] underscored that trust is the cornerstone of impactful mentorship. "Effective mentorship hinges on trust and honesty. It's about creating a relationship where open communication is not just encouraged but is foundational," she said. Building trust through curiosity, active listening, and understanding creates a safe space where mentees feel supported and understood. This trust enables mentors to provide personalized advice that resonates deeply.

One key insight from these conversations was the vital role of authenticity in mentorship. DiFerdinando emphasizes that effective mentorship relies on honesty and transparency. "Show young women the possibilities…being honest, it's not always easy, but sharing your story and lessons learned makes a difference because it's not all about successes; it's about the journey,"[17] she explained. By openly discussing both her achievements and challenges, DiFerdinando fosters a relatable and impactful learning experience. Her approach helps mentees build resilience and gain valuable insights into the realities of career growth.

Another critical component of effective mentorship is offering precise, actionable feedback. Robertson explained how tailored advice helps mentees focus on areas for improvement and build their confidence. "It's about more than just saying 'good job'; it's about saying, 'here's what worked, here's what didn't, and here's how you can improve.'" By listening carefully to their aspirations and delivering targeted guidance, mentors like Robertson provide a clear road map for growth.

While mentorship plays a vital role in guiding and shaping your career, there's another dynamic that can be even more critical: sponsorship. Unlike mentors, who provide advice and support, sponsors actively advocate for you, leveraging their influence to ensure your name is considered for key opportunities and advancement.

Chilazi, highlights this critical distinction: "Women often receive plenty of advice and guidance but lack the advocacy that comes with sponsorship. This means they might be well-prepared but still miss out on key opportunities because no one is pushing for them at the decision-making table."[18]

Sponsorship

Sponsorship is one of the most transformative yet misunderstood dynamics in career advancement. While mentorship provides guidance and support, sponsorship goes a step further—ensuring that your name is heard in rooms where decisions are made. Throughout my conversations with leaders, one theme was clear: sponsorship requires focus, trust, and a willingness to advocate for others. However, the paths to finding and cultivating a relationship with a sponsor are as diverse as the leaders themselves.

One glaring disparity that emerged is the gap in sponsorship opportunities between men and women. Men are 46% more likely to have a sponsor[19]—a statistic that significantly impacts their career progression. As Chilazi, explains, "This gap in sponsorship contributes to the slower career progression of women, despite often having similar or even superior qualifications and experience compared to their male counterparts."[20] Bridging this gap is critical to leveling the playing field and ensuring women are recognized and advanced based on their talents and contributions.

Leaders I spoke with shared a range of perspectives on what sponsorship looks like and why it's essential. Sylvia Ann Hewlett, in her groundbreaking book *Forget a Mentor, Find a Sponsor*[21], offers a succinct explanation: "Mentors are those people who take an interest in counseling you because they like you, or because you remind them of themselves. Sponsors, on the other hand, invest in your career because they see your advancement as beneficial to their own goals, organization, or vision."

A sponsor isn't just a supporter—they're an active advocate. They champion your work at decision-making tables, advocate for promotions and pay raises, and provide "air cover" that allows you to take risks safely. Jennika Gold, Chief Operating Officer and Co-founder of Isle Data,[22] summarizes it best: "Having a sponsor in the organization—somebody who can be in the room when these impactful decisions are being made—is crucial for career advancement."

Despite the importance of sponsorship, women often struggle to access it. Sponsorship tends to thrive in informal, unstructured settings—golf outings, exclusive dinners, or social networks where women, particularly women of color, have historically been underrepresented. Asha Keddy, former corporate VP at Intel,[23] likens breaking into these networks to joining a tight-knit club: "Most boardrooms or senior-level discussions are composed of people who've known each other for years. You have to work extra hard to be visible, to show why you belong there."

How to Find and Cultivate Sponsors

Sponsorship doesn't happen by accident. While mentors might come naturally through relationships or formal programs, sponsors are often harder to find and cultivate. As many leaders I've spoken with shared, sponsorship requires deliberate effort—on both sides.

Sponsors want to back winners. They look for individuals with a proven track record of delivering results and demonstrating potential. Your performance matters. Take on high-visibility projects that showcase your abilities. For example, if your company is launching a new product, volunteer to lead a critical initiative or propose innovative solutions. Consistently exceeding expectations makes potential sponsors take notice. Remember, they're putting their reputation on the line for you, so give them plenty of reasons to feel confident.

Manju Abraham's experience illustrates this perfectly. Her strong performance and visible contributions led her VP to recognize her potential. "My VP at that time acted like a sponsor to me because he took me along when he took on a new role. He must have seen something in me,"[24] she reflects. Now, as a leader, Abraham is committed to paying it forward by supporting women, ensuring they receive well deserved opportunities and recognition.

Similarly, Denise Lee Yeh, Vice President of Engineering at Cisco, shares how a male sponsor played a pivotal role in shaping her career. "I was brave enough to walk through the doors that he opened," she recalls. Through those opportunities, she not only gained critical skills but also developed her leadership style. "His sponsorship helped me land big stretch assignments, which ultimately led to even more opportunities of increasing responsibility," she explains. Her story underscores how sponsorship doesn't just open doors—it accelerates growth by placing you in situations that stretch your capabilities.

So, where can you connect with potential sponsors? Get into the rooms where decision-makers are present. Attend leadership meetings, volunteer for cross-functional projects, or contribute to company-wide initiatives. Think strategically about where you can showcase your value. And don't overlook informal settings—one friend of mine, now a VP at a major tech company, met her first sponsor at a charity fundraiser. That casual connection turned into a game-changing relationship.

Be intentional about visibility. Wall Street veteran Carla Harris advises: "Figure out who has a seat at the decision-making table...make sure they have visibility into your work...and build relationships with two or three of those individuals." Once you've identified a potential sponsor, approach the conversation with clarity and respect. Clearly articulate your career ambitions and how their sponsorship can support your goals. Frame the request around mutual benefit—how your success contributes to their objectives or the broader success of the organization.

Deepna Devkar, SVP of Machine Learning Engineering and AI, Global Streaming at Warner Bros. Discovery,[25] adds an interesting perspective on sponsorship: "Sponsors don't necessarily have to be people in higher positions; they can be members of your own team, even those who report to you. I think a common mistake is assuming that a sponsor should always be someone you look up to or someone in a more senior role." Devkar believes that a leader's success is largely determined by the success of their team.

Anuradha Dodda, Head of Engineering/CTO, Content Technology Group at Thomson Reuters[26] with more than 26 years of experience in tech, found herself in a different situation. "I never had that luck, to be honest. Nobody ever came to me and gave me the [sponsorship] opportunity," she shared. Instead of waiting for someone to push her forward, Dodda took the initiative herself, saying, "Hey, I think I can do this job.

Tell me how can I help you?" Her proactive approach helped her create her own opportunities, proving that sometimes you have to advocate for yourself rather than wait for sponsorship.

Sponsorship isn't a "set it and forget it" deal—you need to nurture it. Keep your sponsor informed about your progress. If you achieve a major milestone, let them know. For instance: "Hi [Name], I wanted to share some exciting news—I successfully delivered [specific outcome] on the [project name]. Your earlier advice was invaluable, and I'm grateful for your guidance." This keeps them invested in your success.

Interestingly, many women leaders shared that they were chosen by their sponsors rather than actively seeking them out. Fern Johnson, former CTO and Vice President, Infrastructure & Operations at PepsiCo,[27] explains, "I'm a firm believer that a sponsor chooses you. You don't choose a sponsor. You can choose a mentor, or a mentor can choose you, but when someone says, 'I want to now sponsor you,' they are leaning in and saying, 'I'm willing to invest in your advancement…'" Linda Yao adds her perspective, "Sponsorship is something that has to be earned. You don't ask for a sponsor; you don't campaign for a sponsor. I've been really fortunate to get sponsors because I did good work." It's about showing your potential sponsors that you're worth investing in.

Whether a sponsor chooses you or you proactively seek one out, the key is the same: consistent results, intentional visibility, and a clear demonstration of your potential.

Diversify Your Sponsorship Portfolio

But what happens if your sponsor leaves the company? Would you still be okay?

Grace Pérez, recalls, "There was a particularly tough moment for me when my sponsor left. Suddenly I felt I didn't have anyone else supporting me in the rooms where important decisions are made."[28] People leave for various reasons, often personal ones—and their departure can leave a significant gap in your support system if you're not prepared.

To mitigate this risk, think strategically like an investor and diversify your "sponsorship portfolio." Just as you wouldn't put all your investments into one stock, you shouldn't rely on a single sponsor. Cultivate relationships with potential sponsors across different levels, departments, or even industries. You want to be in a position where, when your sponsor moves on, other leaders want to fill the gap because they have seen the impact you are making. Your sponsor often can help with this transition. This level of preparedness ensures continuity in your support network and expands the range of opportunities available to you.

The truth is, sponsors don't need to be your role models. You don't even need to admire their leadership style or share your deepest concerns or secrets with them. Ideally, they are in a position of power and influence to help you get where you aspire to go.

Being a Sponsor

Consider stepping into the role of a sponsor yourself. While it might appear that the protégé, often referred to as a "sponsee," is the primary beneficiary, sponsorship is just as transformative for the sponsor. It's an opportunity to shape the careers of others while also cementing your legacy as a leader (we'll dive deeper into legacy-building in Chapter 10). When grounded in trust, transparency, and honesty, sponsorship becomes a mutually rewarding partnership that drives growth for both individuals and the organization.

So, why is being a sponsor so important? Exceptional leaders understand the value of building and leading high-performing, adaptable teams (we'll discuss this further in Chapter 6) and nurturing the next generation of leaders. By investing in the development of future leaders, you're not just supporting an individual's career—you're ensuring your organization has a pipeline of capable, forward-thinking professionals ready to take on greater responsibilities. This kind of investment ultimately fosters organizational resilience and long-term success.[29]

Siri Chilazi, previously introduced as a senior researcher, Women and Public Policy Program at Harvard Kennedy School, is also the co-author of *Make Work Fair* and has been instrumental in advancing the concept of microsponsorship. As Chilazi puts it, "Microsponsorship is great because it doesn't require much extra time, no training, no big formal program. As a senior leader, think about how you can uplift other people—of course, people who are competent, capable, deserving, who have done the hard work." She adds, "We all can do it [microsponsorship] every day…providing visibility to the people who are working underneath you or the more junior people who are, you know, doing the work behind the scenes."[30]

Microsponsorship is an accessible, actionable way for leaders to elevate their team members and foster growth. This might involve suggesting someone's name for a promotion, connecting them with senior stakeholders, or nominating them for a professional development program.

Sponsorship propels others forward, but lasting change requires a culture of support. Securing a sponsor is only possible with intentionality, visibility, and persistence. Leaders who see your contributions and ambition will eventually advocate for you if you steadily deliver results. In the next section, we'll explore how allyship amplifies this impact by creating environments where diverse voices thrive.

Allyship

Everyone talks about the importance of allyship and "finding your people," but for women in tech, this is often easier said than done. How many times have you heard someone say, "Just reach out," only to feel dismissed or overlooked? Women in tech don't just need any connections; they need true allies who show up with intent, commitment, and a readiness to disrupt the status quo. Allies can be mentors, sponsors, colleagues—anyone who's willing to stand beside you and advocate for change not only when it's easy or convenient but especially when it's the most needed. Male allies are crucial, especially in male-dominated industries like tech.[31] Female allies supporting women is equally powerful. It's about creating a network of support where we lift each other up rather than competing for the lone "woman's spot" at the table. Research confirms that having at least one ally in the workplace nearly doubles the likelihood of employees being satisfied with their job, feeling connected to their work culture, and experiencing a sense of belonging within their organization.[32]

As Monique Jeanne Morrow, a global technology leader and President and Co-founder at The Humanized Internet,[33] aptly said, "Women often feel they have to scratch and fight to get to their positions. Being an ally means using your influence to open doors for others and advocate for their advancement." Nadine Thomson, President, Product Deployment & Operations, Choreograph,[34] has experienced the impact of male allies firsthand. Reflecting on her own career, she shared that early male sponsors and advocates pushed her to take on new roles and challenging projects. "I owe a lot of my career to male allies.... They weren't thinking about it as a male-female thing, but they ended up advocating for me in ways that had a lasting impact," she explained.

Thomson believes that achieving real change in tech requires men to step up with the same level of commitment. "The real change happens when men see getting more women into tech as a priority.... Without this, we'll simply nibble around the edges of this challenge for decades," she emphasized.

What does allyship look like in action? It's not just about grand gestures—although they can be impactful during key decision-making moments—but about consistent, everyday behaviors. True allies are those who call out bias, advocate for your promotion when you are not in the room, and provide mentorship and support when it's most needed. In meetings, for instance, this might mean a colleague redirecting credit to you when someone attempts to claim your idea or stepping in to ensure your voice isn't overshadowed by interruptions. Over time, these seemingly small acts contribute to building an environment where women can truly thrive.

Elaine Montilla, she was introduce earlier in the chapter[35] experienced countless microaggressions throughout her career. "Having a network of allies, especially male allies, helped me regain my confidence," she told me. "There were times when they would call out biased behavior on my behalf, and that made all the difference. It wasn't just about me fighting my battles alone."

Building Your Network of Allies

So, how do you find and build your network of allies? It starts with advocacy, openness, and reciprocity. Advocate for others, and they'll likely do the same for you. Be open about your challenges, and you might find that others are willing to step in and support you in ways you didn't expect. Remember, allyship is a two-way street. Being an ally to others creates reciprocal relationships that benefit everyone.

Allies don't always have to be in positions of power. They can be colleagues, mentors, friends, or even mentees. What matters is that they support you and help you navigate the complex world of tech. Sometimes, their role becomes crucial in the context of important meetings.

Swetha Kolli shared a smart approach for turning colleagues into allies: have a "meeting before the meeting." This involves connecting with key colleagues ahead of big discussions, especially those who'll be in the room, and gaining their support for your ideas. Kolli explained how she even suggests specific ways for allies to contribute during the meeting, ensuring her ideas have backing when it matters most.[36] This simple but effective strategy helps build support and amplifies your voice.

People ally with others for various reasons. Often, shared values draw people together—whether it's a commitment to diversity, innovation, or simply a mutual goal of helping others succeed. To tap into this, be vocal about your values and goals, allowing others to see what drives you. When people recognize their own values reflected in yours, they're more likely to step up as allies.[37]

Creating a Personal Board of Advisors

Throughout my career, I've been fortunate to build a network of mentors, sponsors, and allies I refer to as my Personal Board of Advisors. This group, consisting of exceptional individuals I've connected with through the WomenTech Network, Founder Institute, Coding Girls, Drupal, and other platforms, has supported me through challenges and celebrated my successes.

What is a Personal Board of Advisors? It's a trusted circle of professionals strategically selected to guide and support you. Think of it as a blend of mentors, who provide wisdom and guidance; sponsors, who advocate for you and open doors; and allies, who amplify your voice and ensure you're seen and heard. Together, they offer diverse and invaluable insights that significantly enhance your leadership journey.

I carefully selected individuals from different areas of expertise—seasoned executives, peers who excel in areas where I wanted to grow, and even junior colleagues who bring fresh perspectives. Regular check-ins allowed us to discuss goals, challenges, and progress. Their honest feedback and varied viewpoints have been invaluable in helping me navigate complex decisions.

Building these relationships requires openness and reciprocity. I made a conscious effort to offer my support when possible, whether by sharing industry insights, providing feedback on their projects, or connecting them with others in my network.

Titina Ott Adams, Chief Customer Officer at RealPage, spoke about this concept at the Women in Tech Global Conference. In her session titled "Building Your Own Board of Directors—The Importance of Networking,"[38] she emphasized the importance of surrounding yourself with people who can offer different perspectives and support your growth. She highlighted how her own board of directors provided her with the guidance needed to navigate her career and achieve her goals. Adams shared specific instances where her advisors helped her make critical decisions about career moves, leadership strategies, and personal development.

D'Lovely Gibson, former SVP, Equifax, also shared her insights during the Women in Tech Global Awards. In her keynote "Building a Personal Board of Directors to Ensure your Growth and Development,"[39] she discussed how having a diverse and supportive network has been crucial to her personal and professional development. Gibson stressed the importance of choosing individuals who challenge you, support you, and hold you accountable. She recounted a time when she was at a career crossroads and uncertain about whether to take a risky job offer. Her board of directors offered varied perspectives, helping her weigh the pros and cons, ultimately guiding her to make a decision that aligned with her long-term goals. This diverse input was crucial in ensuring that her choice was well-rounded and considered all possible impacts on her career.

Being an Ally

Allyship isn't just about others helping you succeed; it's about using your success and influence to create opportunities for others. As Sandy Carter said, "Always reach back and pull someone forward...that was really important and very impactful to me."[40] Being an ally is about taking action to drive lasting change. It's ensuring that as we rise, we lift others with us, paving the way for the next generation of leaders.

Being an ally also means addressing inequities head-on. When hiring processes unintentionally exclude diverse candidates, an ally advocates for more inclusive practices. When a comment or joke crosses the line, an ally speaks out, ensuring that the workplace remains respectful and welcoming. These moments of action define allyship—they aren't always easy, but they are always necessary.

It is also about regularly asking yourself, "How can I use my privilege to create opportunities for someone else today?" Sometimes it's about championing equal pay or nominating someone for a leadership role. Other times, it's simply making someone feel seen, valued, and included in everyday interactions. These seemingly small moments, when multiplied, create a workplace where everyone can thrive. By committing to allyship, we build a tech industry where everyone can rise together. So, the question isn't if you can be an ally—it's how you will take action today.

As we wrap up this chapter on mentorship, sponsorship and allyship, let's take a moment to reflect on the incredible power these relationships hold. Time and again, I've seen how a mentor's thoughtful guidance, a sponsor's strong endorsement, or an ally's steady encouragement can unlock opportunities, build confidence, and completely transform a career path. These moments can change everything.

Success isn't about breaking the glass ceiling for yourself. It's about clearing the shards so others can follow without fear of being cut. Because success worth having is never a one-person journey. In the end, we're all in this together, and trust me, the view from the top is even better when you've helped someone else get there too.

- **Create a Relationship Map**: The majority of employees are reporting greater satisfaction when supported.[41] List your current mentors, sponsors, and allies. Identify gaps—where do you lack support, and who can you reach out to bridge those gaps?
- **Evaluate Your Mentorship Network**: With mentors, promotions are 5 times more likely.[42] Use the MOSAIC framework to identify missing mentorship roles and seek individuals to fill them.
- **Pinpoint Potential Sponsors**: Sponsors are vital for career growth, yet men are 46% more likely to have them. Identify influential leaders and build connections by contributing to their projects and sharing your achievements in measurable terms.
- **Build Your Personal Board of Advisors**: Personal advisory boards improve business and career outcomes by 24%.[43] Choose six to eight leaders whose expertise inspires you and build relationships for guidance and accountability.
- **Extend and Reciprocate Allyship**: Employees with at least one ally are 1.9[44] times more likely to feel a sense of belonging within their organization. Amplify a colleague's contributions, advocate for them, or create opportunities while reflecting on how you can give back.
- **Stay Intentional and Consistent**: Building strong mentorship, sponsorship, and allyship relationships requires effort and engagement. This month, take one action—reach out to a mentor, offer support to a colleague, or advocate for someone's growth.

6

Leadership Skills, Styles, and Leading Teams

As women, we need to shift from thinking "I'm not ready to do that" to thinking "I want to do that—and I'll learn by doing it."
—Melinda Gates[1]

When I first began exploring what truly makes a great leader, I was captivated by the unique qualities women bring to leadership roles—qualities often overlooked or undervalued.

In conversations with senior executives, and trailblazers across various industries, I asked:

- What are the must-have leadership skills that make a great leader?
- How would you describe your leadership style, and how has it evolved over the years?

Their responses were as varied as their backgrounds. From seasoned CIOs navigating global transformations to startup founders breaking new ground, each leader shared personal stories of challenges faced, lessons learned, and insights gained. Yet common themes emerged.

They spoke passionately about the power of empathy—truly understanding and connecting with their teams. Adaptability surfaced as crucial, highlighting the importance of navigating change with grace and resilience. Authenticity was another consistent message; leading with integrity and staying true to oneself builds trust and fosters genuine connections. Strategic thinking and the ability to inspire through a compelling vision were also identified as essential components of effective leadership.

One thing became clear: there is no single "right" way to lead. Leadership is as diverse as the women who step into these roles. It evolves over time, shaped by our experiences, values, and the unique needs of our teams.

In this chapter, we'll delve into these core competencies and explore the various leadership styles that emerged from these enlightening conversations. We'll examine how these skills interconnect and how leaders blend different approaches to meet the demands of their roles. As we journey through these insights, I invite you to reflect on your own leadership path.

Whether you're stepping into a leadership role for the first time or you're a seasoned leader looking to grow further, consider how these perspectives can guide your development. Think about how you can cultivate a leadership style that aligns with your values and strengths, and that resonates with and empowers those around you.

Core Leadership Skills

At the heart of effective leadership are core skills that transcend any single style—visionary thinking, empathy, effective communication, adaptability, collaboration, authenticity, and executive presence. These foundational competencies enable us to inspire and guide our teams, intertwining with the various leadership styles we might adopt.

Think of it this way: our leadership style is the "how," and these core skills are the "what" that make the "how" possible. They equip us to adapt our approach based on the situation and our team's needs.

Before we get to the leadership styles, let's dive into these essential skills and explore how they not only stand on their own but also enhance the various leadership styles we adopt. By understanding and developing these competencies, we can become more versatile and effective leaders, ready to navigate any challenge that comes our way.

Visionary Thinking

Visionary thinking allows us to anticipate future trends and rally others around a compelling vision. Consider Whitney Wolfe Herd, founder of Bumble, who envisioned a dating platform where women take the lead. This concept challenged traditional norms and tapped into cultural shifts around empowerment and inclusivity. Herd's ability to identify trends in technology and social dynamics allowed her to craft a vision that resonated with millions worldwide. By fostering a collaborative and emotionally intelligent environment, she aligned her team with this mission, turning an innovative idea into a thriving global platform.

When we combine bold, future-focused thinking with curiosity, continuous learning, and adaptability, we cultivate visionary thinking that inspires our teams not just to imagine the future but to create it.

Strategic and Systems Thinking

Strategic thinking involves breaking ambitious goals into actionable steps, while systems thinking helps us see the interconnectedness of our teams, organizations, and industries. Together, these skills enable us to align short-term actions with long-term objectives.

As Bhawna Singh, CTO, Customer Identity at Okta[2] explains, "I'm not just thinking how my engineering team can succeed. I'm thinking how we can all succeed together by aligning with the business strategy and ensuring that our technical goals support the company's overall objectives." This alignment fosters unity and ensures team efforts contribute meaningfully to long-term success.

To build your strategic thinking muscles, focus on seeing the big picture, asking the right questions, analyzing data, solving problems, staying adaptable, communicating clearly, reflecting on what works, and always learning.

Empathy and Emotional Intelligence

Empathy allows us to understand our team members on a deeper level, inspiring trust and collaboration. Emotional intelligence enables us to manage our own emotions and respond effectively to others.

I recall talking with Reetal Pai, Executive Vice President, Chief Information Officer at Teichert,[3] who shared a pivotal moment in her leadership journey. She said, "I started to see how much a leader can impact somebody's emotional well-being. That really changed the dial for me." Recognizing her influence on her team, she prioritized creating a space where people felt seen, heard, and supported.

To build empathy, practice active listening, seek to understand others' perspectives, and acknowledge their emotions. Combine this with emotional intelligence by managing your own feelings and staying composed under pressure, strengthening trust and team dynamics.

Effective Communication

No matter how innovative our vision is, it won't go anywhere if we can't communicate it effectively. Communication connects with people, builds trust, and inspires action.

Linda Yao, COO and Head of Strategy, Solutions and Services Group, Lenovo[4] highlights the power of repetition: "Say it once to introduce the idea, repeat it to reinforce, and then say it again to make sure it sticks. Repetition is what makes the message really land."

Clarity is equally important in effective communication. Breaking down complex decisions into simple, digestible insights ensures that everyone stays aligned and on the same page. When messages are clear and easy to follow, it's easier for teams to build consensus and act decisively.

But communication isn't just talking—it's listening, too. As Vivienne Wei, COO, Data, AI, Tableau and Mulesoft Technology at Salesforce[5] puts it, "Listening…is about expanding our perspectives and understanding what you didn't understand before." Active listening helps us connect with our team, create a common language, and make people feel heard.

Fern Johnson, former CTO and VP, Infrastructure & Operations at PepsiCo,[6] offers a practical tip: "Soft socialization is a very effective way to bring others along before you have to make a decision." Informal conversations allow us to test ideas, gather feedback, and build alignment before formal presentations, making decision-making smoother.

Similarly, I spoke with Nirmal Srinivasan, Senior Director of Engineering for Payments, Digital Wallets, and Tokenization at JPMorgan Chase & Co.[7] Early in her career, she received feedback that her tone and approach came across as "too pushy" or "too aggressive." Recognizing that perceptions matter, especially in leadership roles, she adjusted her communication style without compromising her passion and values.

Instead of leading with directives, she began by acknowledging others' contributions: "I appreciate the work you've put into this approach, and I'd like to build on that foundation. Here's a perspective we could consider to refine it further." This shift fostered collaboration and ensured her ideas were heard and valued.

Effective communication is the bridge between vision and execution. By reinforcing key messages, simplifying complexity, and actively listening to others, leaders can build trust, foster collaboration, and create alignment. In dynamic environments, these practices ensure that ideas connect with people and drive action.

Adaptability and Resilience

Resilient leaders remain calm, curious, and flexible, finding ways to pivot without losing sight of their goals.

Nadine Thomson, President, Product Deployment & Operations, Choreograph,[8] explains: "You need to think about the power dynamic in the room and how you position yourself." This awareness helps us adapt effectively, balancing consistency and self-awareness even when things are constantly shifting. She adds, "Age and experience give you confidence, but it's important to project that confidence even before it's fully there. Faking it until you make it, just pretending you have the confidence until you develop it."

In my own journey, embracing a growth mindset has been foundational to resilience and adaptability. Lori Nishiura Mackenzie, Co-founder at Stanford VMware Women's Leadership Innovation Lab,[9] described it: "One of the most important skills for a leader to have is a learning orientation or growth mindset. The minute we think something is fixed or inherent, we stop doing the practices that are aligned with its success." If we approach challenges with the mindset of "I can learn from this," every obstacle becomes an opportunity.

This perspective is vital in tech, where inevitable challenges demand adaptability. Carol Dweck's research[10] demonstrates that individuals with a growth mindset are more likely to achieve their goals because they view setbacks as chances to learn and grow.

Collaboration and Inclusivity

Collaboration drives strong leadership. It means active listening, sharing ideas, and integrating different perspectives into a cohesive plan. When teams collaborate effectively, they tap into collective brainpower, uncovering innovative solutions that wouldn't emerge from one person alone.[11]

Maria B. Winans, Chief Marketing Officer at Kyndryl,[12] adds, "By fostering an inclusive culture where every team member is empowered to contribute, we unlock creative potential that drives impactful solutions." When people feel respected and valued, they engage fully, investing their energy and creativity.

Leading with collaboration and inclusivity transforms teams, creating an environment where innovation thrives and everyone feels part of the journey.

Authenticity and Integrity

Authenticity inspires trust by aligning actions with values, while integrity ensures leaders remain consistent and principled.

Rebecca Gasser, Partner and Global Chief Information Officer, FGS Global,[13] reflects: "People often tell me, 'You're not what I expected you to be. You're easy to talk to.' And that builds trust right away because I'm being authentic." By staying true to herself and avoiding traditional molds of what a CIO should be, Gasser has cultivated an environment where her team feels safe and supported.

As we explored in Chapter 3, authenticity is not about perfection—it's about embracing who you are, including your strengths and vulnerabilities. Leaders who are authentic inspire trust and loyalty by being transparent, consistent, and approachable, creating teams that feel safe to take risks, share ideas, and collaborate openly.

Executive Presence

Inspiring confidence, earning trust, and holding attention all stem from executive presence—it's how you carry yourself and connect with others. Interestingly, executive presence often reflects not just the leader's qualities but also how others perceive them.[14] Research[15] shows that confidence, communication, and appearance shape these perceptions, highlighting the importance of both authenticity and understanding the expectations of your audience.

Parna Sarkar-Basu, Founder of Brand and Buzz Consulting,[16] puts it this way: "When we talk about executive presence, it's really conveying credibility. Whether it's writing for publications, sharing insights on LinkedIn, or in-person interactions, it's showing, not telling, your expertise." It's not enough to claim we're experts—people need to see it in how we show up, how we speak, and how we share our ideas.

She also mentioned, "Often, executives think they know their material, but when we put them in front of the camera or record them, they realize the message isn't coming across as intended." Watching yourself on video can be transformative. It reveals how you're connecting with your audience and where adjustments are needed to ensure your message lands effectively.

Executive presence isn't just a skill; it's a practice of aligning your authenticity with the impression you leave on others. By refining your communication, seeking honest feedback, and continuously evolving, you can ensure your presence inspires confidence and strengthens trust.

Exploring Leadership Styles

While there are many different leadership styles—including some you'd want to avoid—for the purpose of this chapter, we'll focus on those that emerged from my interviews with remarkable women leaders in tech. Understanding the different styles can help us become more effective in our roles. Throughout these conversations, I've noticed that while each leader has their unique approach, they often blend multiple styles to navigate the complexities of their environments.

- **Transformational Leadership**: Inspires and empowers individuals to exceed expectations through vision and innovation.
- **Servant Leadership**: Prioritizes the needs of the team above the leader's own, fostering a supportive and empowering environment.
- **Inclusive Leadership**: Emphasizes valuing diversity and ensuring all team members feel respected and included.

- **Authentic Leadership**: Grounded in being true to oneself and leading with integrity and transparency.
- **Holistic Leadership**: Considers the organization as an interconnected whole, integrating various aspects to achieve balance and synergy.

While each of these styles has its distinct characteristics, they all draw upon the core leadership skills in different ways.

Transformational Leadership

Transformational leadership thrives on empowering people to exceed their expectations, turning bold visions into practical realities. It's a style that inspires innovation, meaningful change, and extraordinary outcomes by blending visionary thinking, strategic action, and emotional intelligence.[17]

Take Melanie Perkins, the Co-founder and CEO of Canva. Her vision of making design accessible to everyone wasn't just groundbreaking—it was a mission that required resilience, adaptability, and strategic thinking. Starting Canva at just 19 years old, she faced more than 100 rejections from investors. Reflecting on that period, Perkins said, "Rejections from investors, rejections from potential team members, rejections from early customers…To build a startup, you have to run against the grain for years."[18]

Instead of letting rejection stop her, she used it as feedback to refine her approach and strengthen her pitch. Her growth mindset and ability to adapt while keeping her vision front and center turned Canva into a global design powerhouse valued at $49 billion, serving more than 200 million monthly active users.[19]

To turn those dreams into achievable plans, Perkins didn't just imagine possibilities—she crafted bold strategies, broke down goals into actionable steps, and aligned resources to make it all happen. This process involved tackling strategic considerations such as identifying emerging trends in design, empowering her team, and defining success metrics for each stage. Strategic thinking kept her vision both inspiring and doable.

Empathy also played a central role in her leadership. Leaders who connect on a human level build trust and foster collaboration. This reminds me of what Manju Abraham said: "My leadership style is inclusive, empathetic, and transformational. The greatest satisfaction comes from seeing team members grow and achieve results."[20] Like Abraham, Perkins valued her team's growth and created an environment where they could thrive.

Similarly, Suman Rao, VP of US Business Technology & Analytics at HelloFresh,[21] emphasized the importance of being an engaged leader who brings people along on the journey. Rao said, "It's about humility, being ego-less, and engaging with the team at every level to explore and reach their potential."

Communication acted as the bridge between Perkins' vision and execution. She didn't just pitch Canva as a design tool—she shared her personal journey and the mission to make design accessible to everyone. This authentic storytelling inspired her team and won over skeptical investors.

Adaptability was another hallmark of her leadership. She navigated setbacks with resilience while staying committed to the bigger picture. Her willingness to adapt her strategy without losing sight of her vision helped her overcome countless obstacles.

In essence, transformational leadership ignites big ideas, unites teams, and turns aspirations into reality. By crafting a compelling vision, mapping a clear path forward, and building authentic connections—just as Perkins, Abraham, and Rao did—leaders create environments where innovation thrives, and remarkable achievements become possible.

Servant Leadership

To take it a step further, servant leadership prioritizes the needs of the team above all else, placing a strong emphasis on empathy and emotional intelligence. Rather than focusing solely on authority or organizational outcomes, servant leaders invest in the well-being, career growth, and success of each individual. This approach fosters an environment where team members feel valued, supported, and empowered to face challenges and achieve their goals.

At its heart, servant leadership is about sharing power, fostering autonomy, and helping others unlock their full potential. It asks vital questions: Are the people you lead growing in confidence? Are they becoming more prepared to lead others and make meaningful contributions?

Fern Johnson, who has more than 25 years of experience, exemplifies this leadership style. Throughout her career, she has consistently placed the well-being and development of her team at the forefront. "I believe I'm there for the people and the organization. My leadership style is all about servant leadership," she explains.

Johnson's approach revolves around empowering her team to take ownership of challenges while providing the support and resources they need to succeed. By encouraging autonomy, she fosters resilience and adaptability— qualities that are also essential in transformational leadership. She offers guidance and tools but ensures her team takes responsibility for problem-solving, enabling them to grow stronger with every challenge they overcome.

Both servant and transformational leadership create a ripple effect. Empowered individuals not only excel personally but also inspire and uplift those around them. Research[22] backs up the effectiveness of servant leadership, showing how it cultivates trust, commitment, and a positive workplace culture. Leaders at Google[23] and Microsoft have embraced these approaches, recognizing that they boost employee engagement and performance.

When leading with a servant mindset, a simple yet powerful practice is to ask: "What can I do to support you in solving this?" This question empowers team members to find their own solutions while reinforcing that you're there to guide and back them up.

By fostering a culture of trust, learning, and autonomy, servant leaders enable their teams to thrive, building stronger, more resilient organizations that excel in the face of challenges.

Inclusive Leadership

Inclusive leadership goes beyond just supporting individuals—it's creating an environment where every voice is valued, and diversity is seen as a driving force for innovation and success. This leadership style emphasizes equity, making sure everyone feels respected, included, and empowered to contribute their unique strengths.

Research indicates that this leadership style isn't just good for people— it's good for business too. A study by Deloitte[24] found that teams with inclusive leaders are more likely to innovate, make better decisions, and outperform their peers. Inclusive leaders exhibit traits like commitment, courage, cognizance of bias, curiosity, cultural intelligence, and collaboration. By embodying these qualities, they build high-performing teams that integrate diverse perspectives and encourage individuals to take risks and think creatively.

I interviewed Anne Carrigy, CIO at Logitech,[25] who emphasized the importance of trust in building an inclusive culture. "Trust doesn't happen overnight—it's built over time through consistent actions. As a leader, showing your team that you've got their back helps them embrace challenges without fear of failure." This kind of trust fosters a growth mindset and strengthens collaboration.

Being an inclusive leader requires intentional effort. It's not just listening to different perspectives—it's amplifying them. In meetings, inclusive leaders make sure everyone has the chance to contribute, especially those who might be hesitant to speak up. Asking questions like, "What are your thoughts?" or "How might we approach this differently?" creates space for ideas that might otherwise go unheard.

Next time you're leading a discussion or project, think about who hasn't had a chance to speak or whose perspectives might be missing. By actively seeking out and highlighting diverse voices, you'll not only promote inclusivity but also enhance your team's creativity and resilience.

Authentic Leadership

Authentic leadership isn't about polished appearances or rehearsed gestures—it's about showing up as your true self. The best leaders embrace both their strengths and vulnerabilities, building trust and forming genuine connections with their teams. When leaders stay true to who they are, they create a space where team members feel safe to do the same. This openness fuels collaboration, sparks innovation, and inspires people to bring their best selves to work.

For Linda Yao, leadership goes beyond making decisions—she focuses on advancing collaboration and creating space for diverse perspectives. She told me, "I always find it to be one of my goals to be the dumbest person in the room because if it's a place of trust, then I find that is often the best way to continue learning and challenge myself with different perspectives."[26] Yao's humility and openness encourage her team to share ideas freely.

Research[27] published in *Frontiers in Psychology* supports the positive impact of authentic leadership. Studies show that it enhances employees' emotional commitment to the organization and cultivates behaviors that go beyond formal job responsibilities, such as innovation and collaboration. Additionally, authentic leadership builds trust, a critical factor in driving discretionary effort and strengthening team cohesion.

To encourage openness, you can set the tone by sharing a bit of your own experience. For example, I recently told my team, "My daughter's been sick, so I've been juggling work and caregiving. It's been a little chaotic, but we're getting through it. How are things going on your end?" Sharing something personal invites others to open up, building deeper connections.

Authentic leaders also acknowledge their missteps and use them as opportunities to strengthen trust. Saying, "That wasn't the right call, and I take responsibility for it. I'd love your input on how we can move forward," models accountability and encourages team collaboration.

By embracing authenticity, you're not only building trust but also enhancing the effectiveness of other leadership approaches. Leading with integrity and genuine care for your team creates a foundation that supports transformational change, servant empowerment, and inclusive collaboration.

Multifaceted and Holistic Leadership

Many effective leaders integrate multiple styles to address the evolving needs of their teams and organizations. A multifaceted leadership approach combines traits such as authenticity, inclusivity, vision, and empathy, adapting to different situations while staying aligned with personal values, team dynamics, and organizational goals. Holistic leadership adds another layer, considering the interconnectedness of these dimensions and emphasizing strategic alignment, personal development, and team empowerment.

Research published in the *Journal of Values-Based Leadership*[28] supports this approach, highlighting how integrating technical, emotional, and strategic dimensions strengthens organizational cohesion and enhances team performance. Leaders who align their teams with organizational goals create purposeful environments, driving both individual and collective success.

In her reflections, Monique Jeanne Morrow, a global technology leader and President and Co-founder at The Humanized Internet,[29] embodies the power of blending transparency, empathy, empowerment, and flexibility. She emphasizes the importance of encouraging open communication, saying, "You want team members to feel they can speak openly." Transparency builds trust and encourages honest contributions. She also highlights the need to celebrate achievements: "We don't do that enough. Take time to acknowledge an individual's contributions." This practice creates a culture where people feel valued.

Empathy is central to Morrow's leadership philosophy. She supports individual growth, even when it means team members move beyond the organization. "You want to help people grow, even if that means they move on," she explains. Morrow empowers her team to take control of their careers by building support networks: "Build your own board of directors, both inside and outside the company. It's having a sponsor, not just a mentor." Her focus on flexibility ties it all together: "Your career is circular, not linear. Learn to let go to avoid frustration."

As leaders progress in their careers, their styles naturally evolve to match their expanding roles and the shifting needs of their teams. Early on, they might rely on directive leadership to establish authority and deliver quick results. As responsibilities grow, they often adopt more collaborative and inclusive approaches to navigate complex dynamics and leverage diverse perspectives. At senior levels, leadership shifts toward visionary and transformational styles, balancing long-term strategy with immediate execution.

Beyond career stages, leaders often find it beneficial to adapt their styles to fit specific circumstances. In a crisis, adopting a more directive approach might be essential to enable swift and decisive action. During periods of innovation, embracing transformational or visionary leadership can spark creativity and collaboration. When navigating change, servant or inclusive leadership builds trust and addresses concerns by focusing on the needs and perspectives of team members. By blending different leadership styles, you can effectively guide your team through various challenges and opportunities.

Next time you face a leadership challenge, consider how your style can adapt to best serve your team and objectives. Leadership thrives on flexibility and growth. By integrating these principles, you can inspire trust, drive innovation, and create resilient, high-performing teams ready to meet any challenge.

Leading Teams

Yes, leading involves managing workflows and delegating tasks, but the real challenge lies in transforming a diverse group of individuals into a cohesive, high-performing force. It's in this blend of unique strengths and perspectives that something truly extraordinary takes shape. Every team has its mix: bold personalities who dominate discussions, quieter contributors who hold back, risk-takers who push boundaries, and meticulous analyzers whose brilliance can sometimes overcomplicate solutions. Balancing these dynamics is far from simple, but it's also where leadership finds its greatest potential.

It's tempting to surround ourselves with people who think and work like we do—an easy way to reduce friction and speed up decisions. But homogeneity stifles creativity, overlooks innovative solutions, and misses the valuable insights diversity brings. Effective leadership requires embracing this complexity and adapting to individual needs.

In today's fast-moving tech industries, leaders must navigate evolving technologies, conflicting priorities, and varied work styles while keeping teams aligned and motivated. The best leaders don't just guide—they inspire, adapt, and create environments where collaboration and innovation thrive, unlocking their team's full potential.

Assembling the Right Team

When I first started building my own team, I quickly realized that the real magic lies in bringing together the right mix of people whose skills, experiences, and perspectives align with the team's purpose.

It all begins with clearly defining what the team is meant to achieve. Are we launching a new product, driving innovation, or streamlining operations? Once we're clear on the mission, we can think about the skills and perspectives needed to make it happen. For example, a product launch might require a balance of big-picture strategists and detail-oriented planners. An innovation-focused team might benefit from bold risk-takers paired with cautious stabilizers who can assess feasibility.

Success doesn't hinge solely on technical abilities; it's also about combining diverse work styles and viewpoints. Imagine a team filled with visionaries—brilliant but scattered, with no one to execute their ideas. Or a group of cautious planners so focused on mitigating risks that they miss out on opportunities. The key is intentionally blending different strengths and creating an environment where everyone contributes meaningfully.

In an interview with Reeny Sondhi, Chief Digital Officer at Twilio,[30] she highlighted the importance of intentional hiring and empowering her team: "My strategy is to hire the most awesome and best people I can. Then I get out of their way because if I'm constantly in their way, they aren't doing their jobs, and I'm not doing mine." For Sondhi, building great teams also means prioritizing diversity from the start. She explained, "When I'm hiring, my instructions to my recruiters are clear: you need to give me as many minority and women candidates as you can at the top of the funnel. Once we get them into the funnel, it's about who is the best candidate for the role. But if I don't even have diversity at the top, then the chances of anyone making it through are much lower."

After assembling the team, setting them up for success is crucial. This starts with clarity: making sure each person understands their role and how it connects to the team's goals. Collaboration should feel seamless. Structured brainstorming sessions and regular check-ins create spaces where even the quieter team members feel empowered to share their ideas.

It's also important to consider not just the team's current abilities but its potential to grow. Great teams are built with a long-term vision, adapting and evolving together. By combining complementary strengths with a commitment to mutual evolution, we lay the groundwork for enduring success.

Building Team Culture: Trust, Psychological Safety, and Collaboration

Creating a thriving team requires more than gathering skilled individuals; it demands a culture where everyone feels valued and empowered to contribute their best. At the core of this culture are trust, psychological safety, and collaboration. Without these, even the most talented teams can falter.

Psychological safety is crucial. It means facilitating an environment where team members feel comfortable speaking up, sharing ideas, and admitting mistakes without fear of criticism or judgment. By normalizing errors, teams can transform setbacks into valuable learning opportunities that drive personal and collective growth. Similarly, when team members feel safe to ask for help or seek clarification—like saying, "Could you explain that again, please?"—it creates a space where curiosity and improvement are valued over perfection. Building trust and psychological safety becomes even more critical in remote or hybrid work settings where face-to-face interactions are limited.

Trust extends beyond open dialogue. Leaders build trust by shielding their teams from distractions and external pressures, allowing them to focus on meaningful work. Leaders who manage distractions and external pressures help their teams remain focused and productive. Providing this kind of support allows team members to channel their energy into achieving their goals, knowing their leaders have their back.

Mutual respect solidifies collaboration. Taking the time to understand how each team member prefers to work—through candid conversations and shared preferences—builds stronger relationships. When trust, psychological safety, and respect converge, collaboration moves from functional to transformative, enabling teams to achieve extraordinary results.

Managing Team Dynamics and Resolving Conflicts

Team dynamics are as challenging as they are critical to success. Each person brings unique strengths, perspectives, and work styles, which can fuel innovation—or sometimes spark conflict. The key is navigating these differences with adaptability and fairness.

When leading a team, you'll encounter a variety of personalities. Some folks take over conversations, while others hesitate to share their insights. For example, conflicts can arise when deadlines clash with someone's need for detail, or when a silent achiever's contributions go unnoticed. Recognizing these dynamics is the first step toward creating harmony.

Conflicts, whether interpersonal or issue-based, are inevitable in any team. The real test of leadership is how you handle them. Reetal Pai emphasized early intervention: "Unresolved conflicts can fester and create a toxic work environment."[31] She recalled addressing a leader's negative attitude that was affecting the team's well-being. While it was tough, her proactive approach not only resolved the issue but also strengthened the sense of ownership within the group.

When conflicts arise, focusing on de-escalating emotions and fostering understanding is essential. Trust becomes the cornerstone of resolution. Active listening and trying to understand each party's perspective make a big difference. Paraphrasing concerns—like saying, "What I'm hearing is that you felt excluded during the discussion. Is that correct?"—can validate feelings and open the door to constructive dialogue. Setting ground rules for respectful communication helps everyone stay focused on solutions rather than letting tensions escalate.

When conflicts stem from unclear roles or competing priorities, clarity becomes the antidote. Leveraging frameworks such as the RACI model (Responsible, Accountable, Consulted, Informed) can help ensure everyone knows their responsibilities and how their work ties to the team's goals. Grounding discussions in data shifts debates from subjective opinions to objective facts. For example, you might say, "We missed responding to 15 client inquiries within the agreed timeframe last month due to unclear ownership. Let's figure out how we can fix this."

Aligning shared objectives is equally important. When teams focus on collective success, it's easier to bridge differences. Redirecting the focus toward mutual goals encourages collaboration: "Our goal is to ensure smoother collaboration and deliver this project on time. How can we work together to make that happen?"

After resolving conflicts, follow-up is crucial. Checking in to ensure changes are effective not only reinforces accountability but also demonstrates a commitment to continuous improvement.

Accountability, Ownership, and Empowerment

Leadership isn't just about having a grand vision—it's also about making sure your team has the tools and structure to bring that vision to life. Clarity and alignment set the foundation for accountability and empowerment, turning individual efforts into collective success.

No matter how cutting-edge the tools we implement are, they aren't solutions on their own. We need to ensure everyone knows how to use them effectively. Centralizing key information, timelines, and responsibilities creates clarity, eliminates confusion, and minimizes disruptions that could derail progress.

Clarity extends to setting actionable goals. Using SMART goals—Specific, Measurable, Achievable, Relevant, and Time-Bound—provides teams with a road map. For example, instead of "Improve team efficiency," frame it as "Reduce project delivery time by 20% over the next quarter by automating manual tasks and streamlining workflows." Precise objectives give teams direction and a clear way to measure success.

Accountability is the natural result of clarity. As Deborah Corwin Scott, former CIO at Harvard Medical School,[32] notes, "Clear expectations lead naturally to accountability." When everyone understands their role and responsibilities, ownership becomes a shared commitment rather than an obligation. Regular check-ins—whether weekly stand-ups or one-on-one meetings—reinforce this accountability and provide opportunities to address challenges and celebrate progress.

Empowerment means granting your team the autonomy and support to take ownership of their work and drive meaningful results. Rebecca Parsons, CTO Emerita at Thoughtworks,[33] described it perfectly: "Empowerment comes from owning the process." She advocates for focusing on outcome-driven goals rather than micromanaging each step. "When team members figure out how to achieve objectives on their own, they grow in unexpected ways."

Leaders who prioritize clarity, foster accountability, and actively empower their teams create a culture where collaboration and innovation thrive.

Giving Feedback

Feedback is one of the most powerful tools in a leader's arsenal. Four out of five employees say they are motivated to work harder when their boss shows appreciation for their work.[34] Done well, feedback can inspire advancement, build trust, and elevate team performance. Handled poorly, it can demotivate or alienate team members. The key is striking a balance between directness and empathy, tailoring feedback to the individual and the situation.

When it comes to positive feedback, timing and visibility matter. Public praise not only motivates the individual but also sets an example for the team. "Acknowledging their achievements shows that their contributions matter,"[35] says Devshree Golecha, Head of Enterprise Data & Business Intelligence at Step Up For Students. Recognizing success in a team meeting or a company-wide announcement can amplify its impact, though introverted team members may prefer more personal, one-on-one recognition. Regardless of the method, the message should always be specific and sincere.

Constructive feedback can be trickier to navigate. While the "sandwich method" (starting with praise, delivering criticism, and ending with praise) has its supporters, research suggests it can dilute the message. A study titled "Sandwich Feedback Method: Not Always Tasty"[36] points out that recipients often focus on the positive comments, missing the critical feedback altogether. A more effective approach is blending empathy with actionable solutions.

The sandwich method can still be effective, but only when used with caution and intention, particularly in scenarios where the recipient is new or painfully sensitive to feedback. A "sandwich with a twist" begins with genuine positive reinforcement, transitions to constructive critique, and ends with collaborative action steps that inspire growth. For instance, you might say: "I appreciate how you've taken ownership of organizing the project milestones—it's clear you're invested in making this a success. It seems some details weren't communicated clearly, which might be why we've encountered delays. How can we ensure expectations are clearer going forward? I'd love to hear your ideas on refining this process."

When leaders overemphasize care but shy away from delivering direct and actionable feedback, they can fall into the trap of what Kim Scott calls Ruinous Empathy. This often stems from the fear of upsetting the recipient but ultimately undermines team performance. Scott's concept of Radical Candor[37] offers a clear framework: caring personally while challenging directly. For example, a leader might say: "I value the expertise and effort you bring to the team. Missing the last project deadline caused a significant delay for everyone, which we can't afford on critical projects like this. Can you walk me through what happened? I want to understand if there were obstacles we missed and explore how we can address them to ensure this doesn't happen again."

This approach avoids sugarcoating the issue. It is about balancing care ("I value your expertise") with directness ("missing the deadline caused delays"). By focusing on the behavior, not the person, it avoids defensiveness and fosters a productive dialogue. By addressing the issue directly, you ensure it doesn't become a recurring problem, while still showing care and respect for the individual. While you might still feel uncomfortable being blunt when doing it, remember that being nice won't solve the issue itself. And in many cases, it would be you or another team member fixing it (again) if not addressed in a timely way.

Tailoring feedback to individual preferences is another effective strategy. During onboarding or regular check-ins, ask team members about their preferred feedback style—whether they prefer written feedback for reflection, verbal discussions, or immediate input. This adjustment can make feedback more effective and ensure it's received as intended.

Creating a safe space for questions is essential. Normalizing statements like, "If you're unclear about how your work ties into the bigger picture, just ask," cultivates psychological safety. When team members feel comfortable seeking clarification, they're more likely to stay aligned and contribute meaningfully, rather than second-guessing or hesitating to speak up.

Throughout this chapter, we've explored the complexities of leading teams: building trust, navigating diverse dynamics, fostering psychological safety, and empowering others to reach their potential. We've seen how visionary thinking, adaptability, and empathy form the foundation of great leadership while intentional communication and thoughtful feedback strengthen its execution. But the real key to success lies in your ability to remain curious, open, and committed to self-improvement.

If this chapter sparked more questions than answers, that's by design—leadership is a continuous journey of self-reflection, discovery, and growth. There's no one "right way" to lead, but there is a way to become a better leader. By embracing your own style, nurturing inclusive environments, and committing to your team's development, you can pave the way for both your personal success and the success of those you lead. Leadership involves evolving—step by step—into the best version of yourself while lifting others along the way.

- **Vision Aligns Teams**: A compelling vision unites diverse efforts. How can you clearly communicate your team's purpose to inspire action and focus?
- **Clarity Enables Accountability**: Only 50% of employees strongly agree they know what is expected of them at work.[38] How can you ensure your team has crystal-clear roles, responsibilities, and shared goals?
- **Empathy Builds Trust**: Emotional intelligence creates stronger team connections. How can you better understand your team's motivations and challenges this week?

- **Psychological Safety Fuels Innovation**: Open dialogue leads to better collaboration. What can you do to make your team feel safe to share ideas and admit mistakes?
- **Feedback Inspires Growth**: 81% of employees work harder when their efforts are recognized. How can you deliver specific, meaningful feedback to your team today?[39]
- **Adaptability Strengthens Leadership**: Resilient leaders embrace challenges as opportunities. How can you approach your next setback with curiosity and a growth mindset?
- **Empowerment Elevates Teams**: Giving teams autonomy boosts engagement and results. What decision can you delegate to your team to encourage ownership and creativity?

7

Negotiating Powerfully for Your Worth

In business as in life, you don't get what you deserve, you get what you negotiate.

—Dr. Chester L. Karrass

We negotiate every single day. Whether it's with colleagues about project deadlines, with our bosses about taking on new responsibilities, or even at home with our family about chores and activities. But when it comes to negotiating for ourselves, especially in our careers, many of us hesitate. We hold back. Why is that?

While the gap between women and men in salary negotiations has shrunk to 4%,[1] women often fear that negotiating assertively might put them at risk of losing a job offer or lead to negative perceptions such as being labeled as difficult, ungrateful, or overly ambitious, which can further reinforce existing stereotypes and hinder professional opportunities. Sometimes it is also because of the fear of damaging workplace relationships.

Moreover, when women do negotiate, they often secure salary increases or benefits that are lower than those negotiated by men.[2] If men ask for and receive slightly higher starting salaries than women, and continue to negotiate more assertively over their careers, the cumulative difference can amount to millions of dollars. This may partly explain why, according to the Institute for Women's Policy Research,[3] women in the United States earn only about 84% of men's median annual earnings. The disparities are even more pronounced for women of color, with Hispanic women earning just 57.5%, and Black women 69.1% of what White men earn.

Have you ever watched someone at work who seems to get promotions left and right, always gets the assignments they want, and exudes confidence—even if they're not necessarily the smartest person in the room? What's their secret?

More often than not, these high achievers know their worth. They understand the unique value they bring to the table and aren't afraid to advocate for themselves. They're the ones who spot gaps in the company, come up with innovative solutions, and create new opportunities. They propose new roles, lead new product lines, or form new teams. They find ways to generate more revenue, reduce costs, or optimize processes—and they get recognized and rewarded for it. They've also faced failures but kept pushing until they succeeded.

So, what does it really mean to "know your worth"?

Simply put, it's a mindset. It's a belief that, just by being who you are, you're inherently entitled to all the great opportunities life has to offer. It's about navigating life with confidence, knowing deep down that you deserve good things. *Your worth is your birthright.* You deserve every opportunity and great thing in life. It's not only about earning them through hard work and sacrifice; it's about realizing that you're already entitled to them.

Now, don't get me wrong—this mindset doesn't replace the need to work hard, skillfully negotiate, advocate for yourself, and deliver results. It's the foundation that keeps you moving forward with confidence. A "healthy entitlement" gives you the strength to take bold risks, to pursue new opportunities, and to trust that you deserve success.

In professional terms, your worth is the value you bring to the table. It's your expertise, your experience, your connections, your network, and your solid track record of outstanding results. It's even the lessons you've learned from your biggest failures—because those experiences have shaped you and made you even more valuable.

Knowing your worth means being fully aware of what you offer. It means backing it up with data and specific examples. Do your market research. Understand industry standards. Get perspectives from mentors or peers in similar roles. Be prepared to articulate your value confidently.

It also means recognizing societal factors that may influence how your negotiation is received and adapting your approach accordingly. Research shows that women often negotiate more successfully when they frame their requests as benefiting others or advancing organizational goals. For instance, instead of saying, "I need a raise," you might position it as, "Increasing my compensation reflects the value I bring in driving team outcomes and achieving organizational goals." This approach aligns personal advocacy with communal values, fostering a collaborative and mutually beneficial negotiation dynamic.[4]

As we dive into this chapter, let's explore how to cultivate this mindset, recognize and express our value, and overcome the common obstacles that can get in the way—like ego, impatience, or not fully understanding our own worth. Our sense of worth is often reflected in what we successfully negotiate for ourselves. Together, we'll uncover strategies to negotiate powerfully for ourselves.

Navigating the Promotion Track

Growing up, I genuinely believed that if you worked hard, were diligent, and did everything on time, your efforts would naturally be noticed. You would be promoted. You didn't need to ask for it. People would obviously notice it because, well, you work *hard*.

I can't tell you how painfully uncomfortable I felt every time I had to make a request on my own behalf. My heart would race, and I'd lose sleep overthinking endless scenarios of what could possibly go wrong and how I might say the wrong thing. It was self-torture. This discomfort I felt wasn't just personal—it was part of a broader conditioning many women face, taught to value being agreeable and putting others first.

There's a lot we need (or have had) to unlearn. Letting go of the "nice girl" behavior that holds us back and normalizing asking for what we want and deserve. And no, it is not selfish.

In a meritocratic world, you wouldn't need to ask for a promotion; you'd automatically be considered. However, the reality in most tech companies and departments is different. Merit alone isn't enough. Success often requires more than just hard work and dedication. It demands strategic negotiation to ensure that your efforts and achievements are recognized, valued, and rewarded appropriately. Overcoming the discomfort of self-advocacy isn't just about navigating unease—it's about confronting fears like rejection, judgment, or hearing "no." So, how do you move forward with confidence and show your worth? Start by building your promotion portfolio.

Strengthen Your Case for Promotion

Before you ask for a promotion there are a few things to consider:

1. **Build Your Track-Record Portfolio:** Create a dedicated folder— call it "My Achievements" or "Success Portfolio." Use this space to collect both small and big wins that highlight your impact. Maybe it's a thank-you email from your boss, a glowing client testimonial, or a note of appreciation from a colleague you mentored. Gather all the evidence of your contributions. Trust me, when you see it all in one place, it's empowering! Look at that list when you feel like you are not good enough or before negotiation day.

2. **Reflect on Your Impact on the Bottom Line:** As you progress in your career, understanding how your work directly impacts the company's success becomes essential. Identify your key contributions and quantify them wherever possible. Ask yourself what metrics demonstrate your impact. For example, have you increased revenue, reduced costs, improved efficiency, or enhanced customer satisfaction? By tying your contributions to measurable outcomes, you can clearly articulate your value to the organization in concrete and compelling terms.

Let's take a look at an example.

You're a product manager preparing to ask for a promotion. As part of your "Success Portfolio," you include the following example: You led the launch of a new software feature that increased customer retention by 15%, translating to an additional $1.2 million in annual revenue. To achieve this, you collaborated with cross-functional teams, managed tight deadlines, and secured stakeholder buy-in. Not only did the feature improve the user experience, but it also positioned the company ahead of competitors in the market.

When reflecting on your impact on the bottom line, you could frame it like this: "My ability to deliver high-impact solutions has directly contributed to the company's growth. For example, by launching the new feature, I helped generate more than $1.2 million in annual revenue, retained 15% more customers, and strengthened our market position. This success showcases my ability to drive innovation and align projects with business objectives."

This example demonstrates your measurable impact, making it easier for decision-makers to see your value and "justify" your promotion.

Yet a strong promotion case isn't just about what you've done—it's about what you're ready to do next. Consider the biggest challenges within your organization. Ask yourself, what significant problem am I excited to solve? And, why should the company invest in me to tackle it? Position yourself as someone who not only identifies issues, but also delivers innovative solutions. Yes, you're smart, talented, hardworking, and dedicated, but framing your contributions through the company's lens—How does solving this problem benefit them?—helps you see things from their perspective. It allows you to present your value in terms of the company's needs and future growth, making a stronger case for why you're the right person to invest in.

Prioritize Promotable Tasks

Promotable tasks are high-impact activities that showcase your leadership potential, strategic thinking, and ability to drive business results. They're visible, measurable, and align with the company's broader goals, positioning you as a key player in the organization's future.

Examples of promotable tasks include:

- Leading strategic company-wide projects
- Mentoring and developing junior team members
- Driving cross-functional initiatives involving multiple departments
- Introducing and implementing new technologies or processes
- Taking ownership of key business metrics and outcomes
- Presenting strategic ideas and progress to senior leadership
- Spearheading innovation and taking calculated risks on high-impact projects
- Building succession plans for team roles or departmental growth

The more you engage in promotable tasks, the more likely you are to advance in terms of pay, performance evaluations, assignments, promotions, and status. Of course, not to mention a deep sense of fulfillment, purpose, and job satisfaction.

You might be thinking, "If these are promotable tasks, does that mean not all tasks are equal?" That's absolutely right. Often, non-promotable tasks—like organizing office events, taking notes in meetings, or handling administrative duties—are things we do out of politeness or because we find it hard to say no. While these tasks are necessary and sometimes even urgent, they don't significantly showcase your leadership potential or strategic thinking.

The term "non-promotable tasks" was introduced by Linda Babcock, a Professor of Economics at Carnegie Mellon University. She and her colleagues found that women are often assigned more of these tasks—duties that are essential but don't directly lead to career advancement. This imbalance can contribute to slower career progression for women compared to men.

Some examples of non-promotable tasks include:

- Organizing office events and parties
- Taking detailed notes in meetings
- Grabbing coffee or running errands for colleagues
- Fixing minor technical issues
- Managing administrative tasks like scheduling or booking rooms
- Coordinating team logistics (like travel arrangements)
- Proofreading or formatting documents for the team
- Volunteering for non-core work that doesn't enhance your leadership skills (like planning birthday celebrations)
- Regularly covering for a colleague's work without recognition or advancement

While being helpful is commendable, overcommitting to these tasks can limit your ability to engage in higher-impact work that advances your career. They often don't demonstrate the leadership, strategic thinking, or problem-solving skills required for promotion.

Instead of only asking, "How can I get to do more to be seen as a top performer?" also consider asking, "What should I stop doing?" Focus your energy on tasks that align with your career goals and showcase your leadership and strategic thinking.

Nadine Thomson, President, Product Deployment & Operations at Choreograph,[5] offers practical advice on navigating these situations. She shared, "In a senior leadership setting, I never take the minutes. I never make tea. That's not because I don't think people should do their fair share, but because it reinforces gender biases." She also suggests tactfully redirecting the responsibility to others, perhaps by positioning them as better suited for the task: "I might say, 'Oh, Alex knows ten times more about this topic than I do,' even if they don't."

Siri Chilazi, a Senior Researcher at the Women and Public Policy Program at Harvard Kennedy School, emphasizes that this "office housework" often goes unrecognized in terms of pay or promotions. She asks, "It's great that you organized the party, but are you getting paid for it? Is it going to give you a bump in your evaluation?" Chilazi suggests that companies should address this issue by hiring someone whose job it is to handle these tasks or by rotating responsibilities among all team members to ensure fairness. "If we have an administrative task, let's hire someone for it, or rotate the responsibility so everyone contributes equally," she advises.

Preparing for a Promotion Conversation

Before you even start this conversation, preparation is key. Know your value by reflecting on your past achievements and how they've positively impacted the company. Align your ambitions with the organization's strategic goals—think about how your skills can help advance those objectives. Anticipate possible questions or concerns from your manager and prepare thoughtful, measured responses. Most importantly, practice active listening. This isn't just a chance to speak; it's a two-way dialogue that can provide valuable insights into what the company needs from you. Sometimes, this reflection becomes a turning point. If you struggle to align with the company's direction, it may be time to pivot to another role or company.

If your manager is open to discussing your future, take this as an opportunity to build a collaborative plan. Together, identify the specific skills, experiences, or milestones that will help you reach the next level. Set clear goals with realistic timelines and commit to regular check-ins to track your progress. This not only keeps you accountable but also allows for adjustments to the plan as circumstances change.

Ask for a Promotion

If I could offer just one piece of advice when it comes to asking for a promotion, it would be this: Don't wait until it's too late. And, whatever you do, try not to start the conversation with something like, "Why wasn't I promoted?" or "I've worked so hard for this." Even if your frustration is totally justified, beginning on an accusatory note can quickly put the other person on the defensive—and that's not where we want the conversation to go, right?

When it comes to promotions, it's not just about the work you've already done; it's about how prepared you are for the next step. Think of it like planting seeds—you don't wait until harvest time to sow your crops. You need to start early, nurturing your growth and ensuring that decision-makers see you as a natural fit for that next-level role when the time comes. Start the conversation months in advance—ideally before formal review cycles. This allows you to gather feedback, demonstrate leadership, and show improvement over time. But you might be wondering, "How do I even bring this up?" I'm glad you asked.

Here's a brilliant strategy I came across from Chris Voss, a former FBI hostage negotiator. He recommends using a calibrated question that not only triggers thoughtful responses, but also steers the conversation toward your long-term goals without putting pressure on your boss: "How can I be guaranteed to be involved in projects that are critical for the strategic future of this organization?"[6]

When you ask, hold a pause—give the person enough time to process the question.

This isn't just a question about your current role or even your next promotion—it's about positioning yourself as a key player in the organization's future. It demonstrates that you're thinking strategically and signals your interest in growing with the company.

Why It Works:

- It's proactive, not reactive. You're not waiting to be selected or expressing frustration about being overlooked. You're stepping up and expressing your desire to contribute meaningfully.

- It shifts focus to future opportunities. Instead of dwelling on past achievements (which, of course, are important), this question opens up a conversation about how you can add value moving forward.
- It triggers a collaborative mindset. By asking how you can be "guaranteed" to contribute to critical projects, you're inviting your manager to work with you on a plan. This shifts the conversation from "Why didn't I get promoted?" to "How can I ensure I'm ready for the next opportunity?" or "How can I grow from Director to VP?"

The beauty of asking this question early is that it gives you time to develop a clear plan. You can build up the succession plan needed for your current role, gather data on your achievements, and align your work with the company's strategic goals. With this proactive approach, when promotion time rolls around, you won't have to argue for why you deserve it. The evidence will speak for itself, and your manager will already see you as the natural choice.

If the person you're asking doesn't have an immediate answer, don't panic. Be prepared with some ideas to guide the conversation. You could say something like:

> I understand that this might require some thought. Based on my understanding of our [company/department]'s current priorities, I see a few areas where I could make a significant impact, particularly in a larger capacity. For example, I've noticed that [specific project or initiative] is coming up on the horizon, and I'd love to take on a leadership role with additional responsibilities in driving that project to success.

If they're unsure or need time to reflect, you can also ask follow-up questions like:

- What do you think the key priorities for the team or organization will be in the next year?
- Are there any upcoming projects or initiatives that you think would benefit from my skills and experience?

If your manager needs more time to think, propose a follow-up meeting to keep the conversation going. For example:

I completely understand that you may need time to reflect on this. How about we touch base in a couple of weeks after you've had some time to consider where I can best contribute? In the meantime, I'd be happy to draft a few ideas for where I see myself growing and adding value.

Positioning Yourself for Success

In my interview with Wendy Gonzalez,[7] CEO of Sama, she emphasized the importance of strategically aligning your contributions with the company's future direction. She explained that when asking for a promotion, it's critical to position yourself as someone who can lead high-impact projects that are central to the organization's growth.

Gonzalez pointed out that this approach allows you to demonstrate not only your readiness but also your understanding of the broader business goals. She said, "Don't let doubt hold you back. I used to think, 'I can only pursue what I've done before,' but that limits your growth. You're not just a culmination of your past experiences—you are your leadership competencies, your ability to drive results, and how you work with teams."

She also stressed that advocating for yourself is essential, particularly when it comes to asking for new roles or promotions. Gonzalez shared a personal anecdote about how it took her time to realize that the worst anyone can say is "no," and that by not advocating for herself earlier in her career, she may have missed opportunities.

"It took me a while to figure out that asking isn't unreasonable. The worst anyone can say is no. And that's okay," Gonzalez explained. Sometimes "no" means "not yet," and sometimes it might be an indication that you should look for another role where you can grow.

Embrace the Possibility of "No"

It's important to understand that hearing *no* doesn't have to be the end of the road. In fact, it can be an opportunity for growth. *No* might mean:

- **Not yet**: Perhaps the timing isn't right, but your manager now knows your aspirations and can keep you in mind for future opportunities.

- **Need for development**: It might highlight areas where you need to develop further skills or experience. This feedback is invaluable for your professional growth.
- **Misalignment**: Sometimes, it may indicate that your current organization isn't the right place for your ambitions, and that's okay. It could be a catalyst for exploring new opportunities where your goals align better.

Embracing "Happy Problems"

What happens when you're promoted without even asking for it? Maybe you weren't thinking about moving up just yet, and suddenly, an opportunity lands in your lap. Perhaps you don't feel entirely ready for the role, or it's something completely new. I like to call these dilemmas "happy problems," but it's also when imposter syndrome can pop in for a visit. Don't be fooled by it.

During a conversation with Penelope Prett,[8] a Fortune 500 Senior Executive, she shared some wisdom from her epic journey. She emphasized the importance of saying "yes" to challenging opportunities, especially those that offer new experiences. It's a strategy for growth and positioning yourself for future promotions.

"I had someone very early in my career tell me, if you're offered a role to do something, and it has any dimension to it of being something you haven't done before—no matter how you feel emotionally about it—don't say no," Prett recalled." The point is, everything you do professionally is going to teach you something. Sometimes you can't get the lessons you need by doing only the things you want to do. You've got to do stuff that's way outside your comfort zone to get the learnings and training that you can't access through your normal path."

Isn't that powerful? It reminds me that sometimes, the best growth happens when we step into the unknown.

When reflecting on her journey, Anne Carrigy, CIO, Logitech shared a pivotal moment in her career. She was offered a tech role managing a technical team. Initially, she declined, saying, "I'm not technically trained. How can I manage that team?" She turned it down multiple times until she was encouraged to take it on.

Despite her initial hesitation, Carrigy eventually accepted the role. It took time, but she realized her value came from bringing a business-oriented perspective to the team. Reflecting on the experience, she said, "We need to be closer as an IT organization to business.... That was where I was bringing value." Ultimately, this role expanded her responsibilities and contributed significantly to her career growth. It's about trusting the person who sees potential in you—they recognize what you can bring to the table.

Then there's Deepna Devkar, SVP of Machine Learning and AI, Global Streaming at Warner Bros. Discovery, who[9] shared a unique challenge from early in her career: she was promoted too early. "I was promoted very early in my career, and to be honest, I wasn't fully prepared for the role," Devkar recalls. The weight of her new responsibilities and managing a team hit her hard, and imposter syndrome began to creep in. "There were times when I felt like I didn't belong or wasn't capable of handling the responsibilities. Imposter syndrome was real."

At first, the transition was overwhelming. The technical expertise that had gotten her noticed didn't fully prepare her for the demands of leadership. But Devkar didn't quit. Instead, she embraced the challenge. Over time, she learned to trust her abilities and make decisions with confidence. "Looking back, being promoted early was a blessing in disguise," she reflected. "It forced me to grow faster and develop leadership skills that I wouldn't have acquired if I had stayed in my comfort zone." That promotion became the catalyst for her rapid growth as a leader, shaping her into the professional she is today.

I love such stories because they highlight how someone out there notices incredible leadership potential early on and promotes women into roles where they can shine.

Negotiating a Raise

During one of my interviews, a leader confided in me, "I was sure I was being underpaid but didn't know how much more to ask for. It felt uncomfortable, and I wasn't confident in my approach." Does that sound familiar? Many of us have felt this way—knowing we're worth more but unsure how to navigate the conversation. It can feel uncomfortable. Scary. Terrifying. So, how do you start a conversation about a raise? By asking for it, armed with data, market research, and confidence.

First, validate your feelings with solid evidence. Use resources like Glassdoor, Indeed, LinkedIn, you can check if the company provides publicly available compensation data for the role. Once you know the average pay for your role, let that be your starting point to figure out what you want to aim for in your salary.

You can try asking for the salaries of people within your company, if possible, especially those in comparable positions. Unfortunately, pay disparities still exist, so being informed is crucial.

Next, compile evidence of your accomplishments and contributions to the company. Think about the revenue you've generated, projects you've led, efficiencies you've created, or any measurable impact you've had. Frame your request as a business case, highlighting how your work contributes to the company's success.

Here are a few ways to approach the conversation:

- "Based on market research, I've found that the average salary for my role is higher than what I'm currently earning. I'd like to discuss adjusting my compensation to align with industry standards."
- "Over the past year, I've contributed to [specific project with measurable results], and I believe my compensation should reflect the value I'm providing."
- "I'd like to explore options to ensure my compensation reflects my contributions and the impact I'm having here."

Remember the philosophy shared by Rebecca Gasser, Global CIO at FGS Global[10]: "It's always a no unless you ask." She explains, "You might hear no, but it's a no if you don't ask." Her recommendation is to start with low-risk opportunities to build your confidence, then gradually take on higher-stakes negotiations. "Then it's not so scary when the high-risk opportunity is presented to you," she adds.

Jennika Gold, COO and Co-founder of Isle Data[11] shared a powerful story with me. She was offered only a 15% raise, despite a significant increase in responsibilities. She knew this offer didn't reflect her market value or the workload she was expected to take on, so she pushed back. In her conversation with the Chief Human Resources Officer (CHRO), she didn't shy away from addressing the imbalance. She recalled saying, "You would like me to do three times as much work for a 15% raise, right?" By framing it this way, Gold clearly highlighted the mismatch between the responsibilities and the compensation offered.

After further discussions, Gold demonstrated how her market value had increased in just six months. "I said, okay, it's only been six months, but my market value is three times what I'm getting paid here." This direct negotiation resulted in the company offering her a significant raise and a bonus. "They gave me a six-figure bonus on the spot and a 30% raise just like that," she shared.

Her story is inspiring, but be prepared for pushback. If a raise isn't possible at the moment, consider negotiating for other benefits like bonuses, additional vacation time, flexible working arrangements, or professional development opportunities.

Also, know your alternatives. Having a backup plan or even another job offer can strengthen your position. If the company isn't willing to meet your needs, it might be time to explore new opportunities elsewhere.

Negotiating a Salary

When I asked a senior tech leader about her salary negotiation experience for a new role, she admitted, "I trusted the company to pay me fairly, and it didn't even occur to me to negotiate. Looking back, I should have asked more questions, but I thought they would offer what's right." This reflects a common mindset—placing trust in employers to provide fair compensation. However, what's "fair" to them may not align with industry standards or your expectations. That's why it's essential to advocate for yourself.

Negotiation advice can come from many sources—books, articles, courses, and conversations with peers. For example, Grace Pérez, former Chief Digital Program Officer at GE HealthCare,[12] shared how she learned valuable negotiation strategies from a speaker at a WomenTech Network conference. Using the techniques below, she secured an extra six figures in total rewards. Her key takeaway? Be specific and get everything in writing. As Pérez explained, "You need to be super clear on the specifics of what you're negotiating.... Women often avoid being too detail oriented because we don't want to be seen as too assertive."

Another strategy she emphasized is "know your worth". Women often undervalue themselves, but "negotiating like a smart woman" involves thorough research and preparation with data to back up your request. Metrics such as increasing team productivity, generating revenue or reducing costs strengthen your case and demonstrate your impact in tangible terms. Equally important is framing your ask in terms of the value you'll bring to the organization. For instance, instead of saying, "I'd like $340,000," you could try, "Based on my track record of designing and deploying a scalable cloud architecture that reduced infrastructure costs by 30%, saving the company $5.2 million annually, and my plan to lead the migration to a more secure and efficient system, I believe a base salary of $340,000 more than aligns with the value I'll deliver." This approach shifts the focus from what you want to what the organization will gain, making your request more compelling (and a bargain for the company).

There's a golden rule when it comes to negotiating a salary: Never make the first offer without asking for a range. I know some companies might try to flip the script. They might insist that you name your salary expectations first or push you to make the first move. But trust me on this—keep asking for the range. You don't want to undersell yourself. Instead, when they press, try this response: "I'm open to discussing a range that aligns with the market value for this role and my experience. Could you share what you're budgeting for this position?" Keep the ball in their court.

Think about it this way: If you throw out a number that's lower than what they were prepared to offer, you've just left money on the table. But, if you aim too high without knowing their budget, you might price yourself out of the opportunity. By getting them to provide the range first, you have a better sense of where you stand and can negotiate more effectively.

Let me share a story of being straightforward in salary negotiations. Deborah Corwin Scott, former CIO at Harvard Medical School,[13] had a straightforward approach when negotiating her salary. When she was offered a position, she boldly asked, "Are you willing to pay me what you paid the last man who had this job?" This direct question not only highlighted potential pay disparities but also opened the door for a candid discussion about her compensation. Her courage helped her secure a substantial salary increase. Corwin Scott's advice is clear: Women must not shy away from asking for what they deserve.

One of the strongest tools in negotiation is leverage, and there's no better leverage than having a competing offer. Share if you have one. Mentioning this creates a sense of urgency and can push the employer to improve their offer to secure your commitment. Having another option on the table shifts the dynamic—you're no longer someone who needs a job but someone they want to hire before someone else does. If you don't have another offer, it's not a dealbreaker, but having one can strengthen your position.

While some leaders mentioned they didn't feel the need to negotiate, trusting that a fair offer would naturally be made, it's important to recognize that advocating for yourself is non-negotiable—especially when starting a new role or taking on additional responsibilities. Employers won't always know or prioritize your value unless you articulate it.

Negotiate Benefits Beyond Salary

While your salary matters, there are additional perks and benefits you can negotiate as part of your new or even current role. Think about the "total rewards"-the compensation you receive beyond your base pay. These may include:

- **Compensation and Financial Incentives:** Equity or stock options, percentage bonus, signing bonus, long-term incentive plans (LTIPs), 401(k) or pension contributions with employer match, financial planning assistance, equity vesting acceleration (in case of acquisition, layoff, or departure).
- **Flexibility and Family Support:** Remote work and/or flexible hours, parental leave, childcare assistance, fertility support (egg freezing, IVF), tuition assistance for yourself or your dependents.
- **Work Essentials and Professional Standing:** Business phone, car, preferred laptop (Apple vs. PC), formal business title and/or reporting line, number of direct reports (to ensure adequate support for your role).
- **Time Off and Well-being:** Paid time off and vacation, sabbatical after a set number of years, mental and physical healthcare coverage, gym memberships, wellness stipends, meditation apps.
- **Growth and Leadership Development:** Executive coaching, professional development (training, certifications, conferences), mentorship and sponsorship programs.
- **Job Security and Relocation Support:** Severance package, relocation assistance, company-sponsored travel and commuting benefits (flights, hotels, or transport reimbursement).

- **Legal and Insurance Protections:** Life and disability insurance, legal assistance, liability coverage for executives.

- **Philanthropy and Social Impact:** Time for volunteer work, charitable donation matching.

If there's a benefit that's super important to you but isn't being offered, suggest it. Some benefits aren't very well promoted or might be tucked away in the employee handbook. After discussing your salary, make sure to get acquainted with all the benefits available. If you find something that's a must-have for you, consider adding a few tweaks to your contract to include your absolute non-negotiables.

Dana DiFerdinando,[14] former Chief Data Officer at GE HealthCare, stressed the importance of reviewing an offer letter carefully before signing, noting that the best time to negotiate is when you're being pursued for a new role. "Make sure you know before you sign your offer letter, because there's no better time to negotiate than when you're being pursued," she said. She emphasized ensuring that the terms are clear, especially regarding bonuses and liability. "If you're given a sign-on bonus, negotiate to ensure that if things go south with the company and it has nothing to do with your performance, you're not liable to pay that back."

Identifying Your Non-negotiables

What are some of your non-negotiables? You know, those things that are absolutely essential for you to do your job well and feel good about your life.

Here are some common non-negotiables shared by leaders I've spoken with, to give you some inspiration.

Company Culture

Reetal Pai,[15] EVP, CIO at Teichert, emphasized that company culture is non-negotiable for her. She mentioned that she doesn't thrive in ruthless environments and seeks workplaces where collaboration and purpose are prioritized. "I've realized that I don't do well in cut-throat cultures.... If that's there, I won't go. It doesn't matter what the price is."

Janet Robertson,[16] Global CIO at RS Group, also stressed the importance of having a good fit when choosing a job. She mentioned turning down multiple offers even when they offered significantly higher pay:

"The one I turned down was almost double the income…. But I knew they weren't right." She made sure the roles aligned with her personal values and must-haves before making any decisions. "When I set out my list of non-negotiables, I wanted to make sure that I didn't short myself on any of them. If it didn't check all of the boxes, then it wasn't for me," Robertson shared.

Diversity and Inclusion

Grace Pérez emphasized how diversity and inclusion are critical factors for her when considering job offers. She expressed that it's important to see real commitment to diversity, not just lip service: "It's whether a leadership team is truly open to what people who may be different from them have to offer versus just looking for a woman to fill a seat." This is especially true in environments where leaders tend to "look and act alike". Her perspective highlights how inclusion and a willingness to embrace diverse perspectives are non-negotiable for her. Similarly, Wendy Gonzalez echoed this sentiment, highlighting that building diverse teams and fostering inclusive leadership are essential priorities for her as well.

To assess whether a company truly values inclusion, individuals can take several steps. Research the organization's track record, such as reviewing reports or examining the composition of leadership teams. Analyze the company's policies and practices, including employee resource groups or mentorship programs. During interviews, ask specific questions about relevant initiatives, inclusive hiring practices, and leadership's approach to incorporating diverse perspectives. Networking with current or former employees and exploring reviews on platforms like Glassdoor can also provide insight into whether the company's culture aligns with its stated values.

Reporting Line

Nadine Thomson pointed out that reporting to the right person is more important than the company itself. She explained that a good boss can shape your career path and improve your day-to-day experience, making this a non-negotiable for her. "The person you work for is more important than the company you work for…. A good boss can actually give you career paths, sponsor you, and make your day-to-day life better."

Time Off

Rebecca Gasser highlighted that paid time off is a critical non-negotiable for her. She stated that it's a key indicator of a company's environment. "I will never sacrifice my time off.… If the company is non-negotiable at, like, say, three weeks, that tells you what kind of environment you're about to walk into."

Always Be Open to Opportunities

In a conversation with Reetal Pai, she shared valuable advice about always interviewing, even when you're not looking for a new role. She explained that men often keep their options open by consistently interviewing, allowing them to stay aware of their market value and be better positioned to negotiate in their current roles.

She recalled how a mentor once told her: "Women never interview for jobs when they have a job. Men interview when they have a job because then they always know their market value and know how much to ask for and negotiate in their current role."

Following this advice, Pai began taking calls from recruiters even when she wasn't looking for a new role, recognizing that it keeps her in tune with industry standards and opportunities. This approach allows her to stay competitive and proactive about her career growth. And really, what's the worst that can happen? You confirm that you're happily employed.

Negotiating Severance and Exit Strategies

Now, let's talk about something that's often overlooked but incredibly important: negotiating your severance package or having an exit strategy.

Many companies offer severance packages across various roles, but you need to negotiate them upfront. I once had a conversation with a C-level executive who shared, "I didn't negotiate my severance when I first joined the company. I assumed that everything would be fair, and honestly, I didn't know how to bring it up without seeming pushy. I've learned a lot since then and wish I had resources like this book earlier in my career."

Negotiating upfront is key, but there's more—you can and should renegotiate when you decide to leave. When you know the value you bring to the company, you're able to negotiate better, especially after delivering stellar results.

One thing is clear: You don't want to wait until you're being let go to figure out what you're entitled to. Clarifying exit terms from the start ensures a fair deal when emotions aren't running high. It's often easier to negotiate severance during your offer stage because both sides are focused on building a partnership, not dissolving one.

When discussing your job offer, ask about severance terms:

- Could you share how severance pay is typically structured based on tenure?
- In the event of a departure, is there a continuation of health insurance coverage, and if so, for how long?
- How does the company handle unused vacation days or other accrued benefits upon departure?

If you work at a company that offers stock options or equity, it's important to negotiate the terms of what happens upon termination. Will your stock vest immediately, or will you lose out on unvested shares? This is especially crucial for employees in startups or tech companies, where equity can represent a significant part of your compensation.

It's also a good idea to decode any new or unclear conditions in your severance package. Many agreements often include clauses about non-compete agreements, non-disclosures, and legal waivers. Make sure you understand the fine print. For instance, does your severance package prevent you from working with competitors?

Janet Robertson emphasized the importance of not waiting too long to exit and having financial security if the company's trajectory no longer aligned with her values. She shared: "You need to have enough money to make an exit. I turned down three other offers before I found the role. If I needed the money, I could have jumped at those, but they weren't the right fit. One company even offered me almost double the income, but I trusted my instinct. On paper, everything looked great, but the CEO's leadership approach didn't align with my values."

Vivienne Wei,[17] COO of Data Cloud, AI, Mulesoft & Tableau at Salesforce, highlighted the importance of negotiating terms upfront, particularly related to stock options. She stated: "Make sure that severance isn't tied to performance-based metrics beyond your control, especially in roles where stock options or equity make up a significant part of your compensation. It's crucial to negotiate these terms at the beginning to avoid losing out later."

The job search process can be long, especially in specialized fields. For most senior management-level professionals anticipate that finding a new opportunity takes 6–12 months[18] on average, reflecting consistent trends over recent years. Having severance helps cushion that gap.

Negotiating for your worth is essential in advancing your professional journey, but the real value lies in standing up for yourself, setting clear boundaries, and shaping your career to align with what truly matters to you. By recognizing your value, equipping yourself with knowledge and thorough preparation, and confidently advocating for yourself, you can achieve your career objectives. Understand your impact, align your goals with those of your organization, and be ready to articulate your contributions clearly. Don't shy away from the possibility of hearing "no"—embrace it as part of the journey toward "yes." Each negotiation, whether successful or not, is an opportunity for growth and a step toward building the career you desire and deserve. Keep your priorities in focus and remain open to new possibilities as you navigate your path forward.

- **Break the Silence on Negotiations**: If you don't ask, you're agreeing to less than you deserve. What bold request can you make today to claim the opportunities or compensation that reflect your true value?
- **Shift from Invisible Work to Impactful Leadership**: Women spend up to 200 extra hours per year[19] on non-promotable tasks. Are there efforts you can redirect toward high-impact projects that showcase your strategic abilities and advance your career?
- **Embrace the Discomfort of Self-Advocacy**: Growth happens outside your comfort zone. Which difficult conversation about your advancement have you been avoiding, and how will you initiate it this week?

- **Negotiate Beyond Salary**: Compensation is more than a paycheck. What valuable non-monetary perks—like flexible hours, professional development, or increased vacation time—are vital to you, and how can you secure them in your next negotiation?
- **Say Yes to Opportunities**: If it scares you, it can help you grow. What ambitious role or project can you accept that pushes you beyond your current limits?
- **Define and Uphold Your Non-negotiables**: Knowing what you won't compromise on is power. What are your top three non-negotiables in your career, and are they being met where you are now?

8 | Resilience, Grit, and Lifelong Learning

I learned to always take on things I'd never done before. Growth and comfort do not coexist.
—Ginni Rometty, former CEO of IBM

In this chapter, we'll explore the three qualities that are essential for navigating the highs and lows of being in tech: resilience, grit, and lifelong learning.

Resilience is your recovery system—how you adapt and bounce back when things don't go as planned. Whether it's overcoming a failed project, a career setback, or a tough challenge, resilience is what helps you stand up, dust yourself off, and get back on track. According to the Workplace Resilience Study, those who love what they do are 3.9 times more likely to be highly resilient.[1]

Grit takes resilience a step further. It means staying committed, driven by the passion behind your work and the determination to push forward, even when progress seems frustratingly slow. As Angela Duckworth, author of *Grit: The Power of Passion and Perseverance*,[2] explains, success is less about talent and more about sustained effort and commitment over time.

And these qualities don't exist in isolation. Lifelong learning is the unifying thread that ties them together, empowering you to embrace change, grow from failure, and discover new possibilities. Through real-life stories, research, and practical tools, you'll learn how to develop these traits and apply them in your leadership journey.

Resilience: Turning Setbacks into Strength

Sometimes life throws curveballs that make us question everything. Back in 2017, after winning her 23rd Grand Slam title, Serena Williams faced one of the toughest challenges of her life. She had just given birth to her daughter and experienced serious complications that could've ended her career. Most people thought she'd step back, maybe even retire, but eight months later she was on the court at the French Open.

Williams didn't return just to collect more trophies; she came back because she believed in her purpose and wanted to inspire others.[3] Her journey reminds me that resilience isn't merely bouncing back; it's showing up, day after day, even when things get unbelievably tough. In tech leadership, our challenges might not make headlines like Williams', but they're no less significant in our lives. Her resilience on the court mirrors the type of resilience many women leaders show in their careers.

As part of my writing journey, I had the chance to interview a seasoned executive and inspiring leader, Maria B. Winans, the CMO at Kyndryl, for our WomenTech Network blog, and her journey is nothing short of inspiring. Maria moved from Chile to North Carolina when she was just 10 years old. Growing up, she often felt like an outsider because of her background, and that feeling followed her into her professional life, all the way to the C-suite.

She told me, "I frequently found myself as the only Hispanic woman in the boardroom. Being in that position was challenging, but I chose early on to lean into the power of being different and to work as hard as I could to achieve all that I aspired to be."[4]

What really struck me was how Winans reframes challenges. She said, "For me, it's not about what keeps me up at night, but what gets me up in the morning."[5] Instead of letting obstacles weigh her down, she focuses on the opportunities to create change and push boundaries. That mindset— seeing challenges as chances to grow—is a real-life example of resilience in action.

Just like Williams and Winans, many of us face hurdles that test our resolve. Whether it's dealing with a project that didn't go as planned, facing a string of rejections, navigating layoffs or industry shake-ups that catch us off guard; it's our commitment to our goals and our determination to persevere that keep us moving forward.

I once shared with a mentee that, while we're not surgeons, the pressure in tech leadership can feel just as intense. The decisions we make impact people's careers, their livelihoods, and sometimes their sense of purpose. When setbacks hit—and they always do—how you respond matters. Will you let it derail your focus, or will you lean into resilience?

Every leader I've spoken to confirmed: resilience is non-negotiable. You've got to build a super-resilient mindset. That means dealing with setbacks, rejections, and yes, failures.

Honestly, I bet that almost every successful person out there didn't hit it big on their first try. We often only see the highlight reel—the successes, the awards, the shiny outcomes. But beneath the surface, there's so much more: the failures, the doubts, the sacrifices, tons of rejections and even more mistakes. Thomas Edison famously said, "I have not failed. I've just found 10,000 ways that won't work."

By focusing on what we can control and pushing forward, we build that vital muscle called resilience. And trust me, in an industry defined by constant change, this muscle is frequently put to the test.

New Environments as a Test of Resilience

One of the quickest ways to build resilience is to throw yourself into a completely new environment—like moving to a different country. It's like hitting the reset button on everything you know. You're out of your comfort zone, adapting to new cultures, possibly a new language, and definitely new ways of doing things. It's challenging, no doubt about it, but it can also be incredibly rewarding.

An inspiring story comes from Ivneet Kaur, the Chief Information and Technology Officer at Sterling.[6] She moved to a different continent not once, but twice! "One of the most difficult decisions was moving to Australia for a senior role at Equifax," she told me. "It was a personal and professional challenge. But I'd already moved from India to the US before, so

I thought, 'Why not try again?'"[7] Each move pushed her out of her comfort zone, but it also made her more adaptable and resilient.

Just like adapting to a new country, working in tech often means dealing with something new. Technologies emerge overnight, projects pivot, teams merge or reorganize—you have to be ready to adapt at a moment's notice. And each time you do, you build up that resilience muscle a little more. Even moving within your own company can be a test of resilience. Switching departments, taking on a new role, or joining a different team—all of these changes force you to adapt and grow. But here's the silver lining: with each challenge you overcome, you become better equipped to handle whatever comes your way, both professionally and personally.

Adapting to Change and Overcoming Setbacks

Resilience is rolling with the punches and making it work.

When the COVID-19 pandemic hit, my daughter was about to turn four months old. Between endless video calls, sleepless nights, and the general chaos, days and nights blurred together. Our team at WomenTech Network was small but ambitious. We had more than 50 events lined up across the globe, and then—just like that—everything was canceled. It felt like the rug was pulled out from under us.

We took a week off to catch our breath, hoping for some clarity. But waiting around wasn't an option. We had to pivot, and fast. We asked ourselves, "How can we keep connecting people safely and still discuss the topics that matter?" That's when the idea hit us: let's take our Global Conference online.

Now, I know virtual conferences are everywhere these days, but back then, it wasn't so common—especially not on the scale we were envisioning. We wanted to bring together 100,000 women and allies in tech. We had planned to have 800 speakers, running multiple sessions across 16 different time zones for three days, an equivalent to 50 full working days of binging empowering and educational content. Ambitious? Absolutely. A little crazy? Maybe.

We rallied our community, and pulled off an incredible event. Convincing sponsors and attendees wasn't easy, but our community believed in our mission. Since then, we've grown exponentially. Today, WomenTech

Network has more than 150,000 members worldwide and is one of the largest communities of its kind.

But here's what people often don't see—the behind-the-scenes hustle. The late nights, the stress, the countless moments of doubt. Late-night calls, working around the clock, solving problems we hadn't anticipated. It's easy to look at our success and think it was smooth sailing, yet the reality is, it took a lot of resilience.

When facing unexpected challenges, the goal isn't just to survive—it's to find a way to thrive. In tough moments, I also recall my mother's advice: "If it were easy, everyone could do it." Remember, every hurdle is an opportunity to reinvent, grow, and ultimately emerge stronger. So next time you're hit with the unexpected, ask yourself: What's the opportunity here? And, What bold step can I take to turn this challenge into a win?

When unexpected challenges arise, the ability to adapt and grow can redefine your career path.

Another compelling example is Nirmal Srinivasan, Sr. Director of Engineering from JPMorgan Chase & Co.[8] Reflecting on her journey, Srinivasan shared, "Throughout my career, adaptability and continuous learning have been my guiding principles. Embracing change and learning from setbacks have been crucial to my growth." Transitioning from forensic sciences to a career in technology was no small feat. Encouraged by her husband, she took on the challenge of learning coding, a skill entirely new to her at the time. Her persistence and openness to learning eventually led her to a thriving career at Netflix and beyond. Her journey underscores the power of embracing unfamiliar opportunities and committing to continuous growth, even when the path is uncertain.

Long-Term Resilience

Anu Bharadwaj, President at Atlassian, highlighted the importance of forming strong connections at work as a key to building long-term resilience. In her keynote at the Women in Tech Global Conference on "Long-term Resilience: How to Manage Your Energy to Manage Your Time,"[9] she shared her initial hesitation about forming close relationships at work. "I was a bit apprehensive about forming friendships at work—what if these close friendships cloud my judgment of them as colleagues and affect my decision-making?" she admitted.

However, over time, Bharadwaj realized that authentic connections were vital for getting through challenging moments. "Being able to form authentic, deep connections is crucial to navigating tough moments," she emphasized. "Having work friends is a big source of resilience for me.... It's important to have a sense of community and togetherness at work."

While professional boundaries are important, the relationships we build at work can become invaluable sources of support that are often essential in managing the demands of a busy professional life. They help us manage stress and sustain our grit over the long haul.

The Grit Factor

When you think of the most successful people in tech, the quality that often stands out is grit. Some might have had early advantages—perhaps they were born into wealth or earned degrees from prestigious places like MIT, Stanford, or Harvard, made connections, and made it. While those things can open doors, grit sustains long-term success, no matter where you begin.

For many women in tech, grit isn't just a skill—it's a lifeline. It's what enables them to turn a "no" into "not yet," to navigate barriers with determination, and to show up every day, believing in the value of their work and the change they can create. As Denise Lee Yeh, Vice President of Engineering, Cisco,[10] reminds us, "People may doubt your abilities, but never let them doubt your determination."

I had an interview with Elaine Zhou, Co-CEO at SageCXO,[11] where she shared how her parents empowered her to tackle challenges head-on. "They made sure that despite the obstacles we faced as a family, I had the best opportunities. They mentally prepared me to be strong," she said. Zhou's story shows how a foundation of mental strength, fueled by passion, can pave the way to leadership. Grit is what drives us to succeed against the odds, not to give up when things get tough—people with grit keep moving, learning, and growing, rising to the top.

Similarly, Reeny Sondhi, Chief Digital Officer at Twilio, mentioned that, "Growing up in India, the value system was about not giving up. My father always said, 'Once you choose a path, commit to it fully and don't turn back when things get tough.' That's where my persistence and resilience come from."

But grit isn't solely inherited or taught; it's cultivated. Even without an early foundation such as learning about it from your parents, grit can be built through deliberate practice—by committing to your goals, leaning on your passion, and showing up every day, no matter how difficult. It all comes down to two things according to Duckworth "the passion and perseverance for achieving long-term goals." Having a knack for something—whether it's tech, leadership, or business—holds value, yet the relentless commitment to growth makes the real difference. Showing up when the going gets tough and finding joy in the process, not just the end result, matters most. She emphasizes that grit is about maintaining effort and interest over years, despite setbacks, challenges, and plateaus in progress.

Think of perseverance as the engine that keeps you moving forward, and passion as the fuel that powers that engine. Passion gives meaning to your efforts. It's what makes those late nights, tight deadlines, and unexpected setbacks worthwhile. It's the emotional connection to your work that keeps you energized and focused. When you believe deeply in what you're doing, you're not just working hard—you're working with purpose. Without passion, perseverance can become exhausting—a mechanical grind that leads to burnout. But when you're passionate about your work, every challenge becomes a stepping stone rather than a stumbling block.

At Founder Institute, we encouraged entrepreneurs to focus on the problem they're passionate about solving, asking, "What challenge would you dedicate the next 10 years to addressing?" This mindset fits tech leaders perfectly—grit means staying committed to a meaningful goal. Solutions may evolve, markets can shift, but a truly significant problem will always call for fresh, creative approaches.

Gritty Leaders

Leaders often face decisions in the fog of crisis or uncertainty, with incomplete information and the stakes high. What separates the merely competent from the truly exceptional is not access to perfect data, but the ability to navigate ambiguity with resolve and purpose. Leaders who demonstrate grit set a powerful example, inspiring their teams to persevere and remain motivated through challenges. People admire gritty leaders; they strive to emulate them and respect their resilience. This is what sets good leaders apart from great ones.

Without grit, however, leadership falters. Indecision and hesitation in uncertain moments signal a lack of confidence, which can ripple through the team. Trust erodes, motivation wanes, and the shared sense of purpose begins to unravel. Over time, this leads to a drift not just in morale, but in the organization's direction and results.

An inspiring example of grit is Manju Abraham, former VP of Engineering from HPE.[12] She faced one of the toughest challenges in her career when her company canceled a major product she was leading—right after a successful release. "We had to let go of a large part of the team," she recalled. "As a manager, the situation was profoundly challenging both professionally and personally." Instead of letting this setback define her, Abraham led with integrity and stayed true to her vision. Her calm leadership enabled her to guide her team through that difficult time and to move forward with confidence focusing more on all the learnings and relationships than on the product itself. She applied those skills with tenacity in a new role and revitalized that organization to innovate and scale. "My efforts were recognized, and within a year, I received the company's highest Leadership Award," she shared.

Lifelong Learning

There's no finish line when it comes to learning. Especially not in tech, where new technologies emerge faster than you can refresh your feed, so staying stagnant is not an option. As Grace Hopper, the esteemed US Navy rear admiral and pioneering computer programmer, so wisely stated, "The most dangerous phrase in the language is: We've always done it this way." Her words serve as a timeless reminder that growth and innovation demand a willingness to challenge conventional thinking and embrace change.

The unpredictable nature of modern careers—marked by layoffs, rapid pivots, or the loss of businesses—can feel destabilizing. Life has this funny way of throwing new challenges at us just when we think we've got it all figured out. And honestly, wouldn't it be boring if it didn't? Growing and learning is a thrilling process. Staying stuck in a cycle of repetitive tasks that no longer stretch your abilities can feel stifling, like wearing shoes that are two sizes too small.

Whether learning a new skill, understanding an emerging technology, or developing a fresh leadership strategy, a commitment to continuous improvement sets successful leaders apart. And this is not limited to formal education. Sure, earning advanced degrees like MBAs or PhDs can help, but lifelong learning is much broader. It involves being open to new experiences, tackling challenges hands-on, and a continuous desire to expand one's understanding of the world. This could mean gaining insights from top experts or immersing yourself in speaking or joining tech conferences such as SXSW, Web Summit, TechCrunch Disrupt, or Women in Tech Global Conference.

A critical component of lifelong learning is seeking fresh perspectives. By surrounding yourself with thought leaders, experts, and driven individuals and tapping into professional groups, you gain access to dynamic learning experiences that go far beyond the pages of a textbook, fostering personal and professional transformation.

Staying ahead in tech means continuously integrating new trends—like AI, cloud computing, and automation—into your skill set. Those who lead the charge into the future are the ones committed to learning. Technologies that were once cutting-edge are now obsolete.[13] Generative AI is rapidly reshaping industries and job roles across the board. Tools like OpenAI's ChatGPT for content creation, Midjourney and Adobe Sensei for graphic design, and Runway ML for video production are transforming tasks once considered exclusively human—writing, designing, and editing—into collaborative efforts between humans and machine. What's truly exciting is how AI is not only changing the landscape but also creating new opportunities for those willing to harness its potential.

Those who adapt to these tools are positioning themselves at the forefront of innovation, ready to boost productivity and make strategic decisions that shape the future of their industries. Developers leveraging platforms like GitHub Copilot are coding more efficiently, freeing up time to tackle complex, creative challenges. In customer support, AI-driven chatbots and platforms like Zendesk and Intercom are streamlining inquiries by providing instant responses and automating repetitive tasks, allowing teams to focus on more complex issues. Marketers using AI-powered analytics tools like HubSpot and Salesforce Einstein can predict customer behaviors more accurately, creating more targeted and effective campaigns.

Practical Strategies for Integrating Lifelong Learning

Between the demands of leading teams, strategizing, and delivering results, where does growth fit in? The truth is, learning doesn't always have to be a massive time commitment. Finding space for growth in the chaos comes down to taking consistent steps, even when they seem insignificant.

Before diving into strategies, take a moment to set clear learning objectives. What do you want to achieve? Whether it's mastering a specific tool, gaining insights into a new leadership approach, or preparing for a future role, having well-defined objectives ensures your learning is focused and actionable.

Here are three strategies designed to meet you exactly where you are—in the middle of your busy day, juggling competing priorities—while ensuring learning becomes an integral, intentional part of your leadership journey.

1. Make learning part of your daily rhythm
2. Apply new knowledge
3. Track progress and reassess learning goals.

Make Learning Part of Your Daily Rhythm A 20-minute podcast during your morning run or a short read over your coffee break can bring fresh insights into your work. Listening to Simon Sinek's *A Bit of Optimism* for 30 minutes while exercising transformed my workouts into dual-purpose activities—good for the body and enriching for the mind. It could be any podcast that resonates with your interests, whether on Spotify, Blinkist, or TED Talks.

I used to make it a habit to read a physical book for 15 minutes. This break from screen time not only rested my eyes but also helped me unwind and ease into sleep. (Later this activity was replaced with book writing!) For some, swapping Netflix binging for a LinkedIn Learning course or documentaries that align with your interests might be the way to go. The trick is to make learning fit into your lifestyle in a way that feels natural and easy.

One effective strategy is incorporating "growth sprints"—dedicated, uninterrupted blocks of time for personal development. For example, you could block off 30 minutes twice a week during your least busy hours to tackle a course module or reflect on lessons learned. Growth sprints allow you to focus deeply on learning without it feeling like a competing priority because there's always something "urgent," "time-sensitive," or "more important." Small doses of intentional learning compounds over time to create significant expertise.

Apply New Knowledge   Learning becomes truly valuable when it leads to action. The key is to integrate what you've learned into your daily work. Maybe you've explored a new tool or method—why not test it in your team's workflow? Whether it's automating a recurring task with AI or streamlining a process, applying new insights helps solidify your understanding and demonstrates their value to your team. Sharing these outcomes in meetings can spark conversations and inspire innovation across the group.

For leaders, this might mean piloting projects where the team experiments with a new skill or approach. For instance, using a framework like the Eisenhower Matrix[14] to prioritize tasks can be a practical way to enhance focus and productivity. After applying these lessons, take a moment to reflect, gather feedback, and tweak as needed.

By actively applying what you've learned, you not only deepen your own knowledge but also set an example that inspires your team to embrace learning as a catalyst for growth and transformation.

Track Progress and Celebrate Growth   How can you be sure your learning efforts are paying off? The answer lies in setting clear, measurable goals and tracking your progress. Whether it's mastering a new skill, earning a certification, or successfully applying a new strategy, milestones turn abstract efforts into concrete achievements. They're proof of your growth and a powerful source of motivation to keep going. And celebrating these milestones is equally important. I've seen firsthand how a simple acknowledgment can inspire incredible momentum. When a team member recently applied an idea from a webinar, I highlighted their initiative in a team meeting.

Personal milestones deserve the same spotlight. When I completed a particularly challenging course, I made a point to share it with my team. It wasn't the certificate itself that mattered (though it's great to share on LinkedIn); it was the act of showing that the effort to learn holds value and that celebrating the journey can be just as rewarding as reaching the destination. Recognizing these achievements—both your own and others'—builds a culture that celebrates growth, fueling motivation, sparking innovation, and driving collective progress.

Get Comfortable Being Uncomfortable

How do you make continuous improvement a habit? Start by stepping out of your comfort zone. Archana Jain, Group CTO at Zurich Insurance Group,[15] emphasized in her Women in Tech Global Conference 2024 keynote, "You have to build a plan where you don't just learn a skill but apply it. Learning without application doesn't stick." Jain also reminds us that true growth happens outside of our comfort zones: "Get comfortable with being uncomfortable when you're learning something new…. That's where growth happens." Her words underscore a universal truth: growth happens in the moments when we feel challenged, even uncomfortable.

You know what else is uncomfortable? Failing. But what if instead of seeing failure as something bad, we would reframe it and see it as a stepping stone, as a breakthrough. I really like one definition of the word fail; it goes "first attempt in trying"[16] and I think it is beautiful. When you take the power from the word *failure* to define you and your journey, you become unstoppable. Reshma Saujani, Founder of Girls Who Code,[17] openly shares on Instagram using #FailureFriday to talk about the things she fails at to help her "build up the bravery muscles."

Like many women in leadership or those on their way there, I often struggled with self-doubt and the feeling that I needed to be perfect before I could take on new challenges. Looking back, embracing discomfort was one of the best decisions I ever made. It led to some of my most meaningful accomplishments and growth—both personally and professionally. Sometimes, we need to remind ourselves that growth comes from pushing through those moments of uncertainty, even when it feels like we're not ready.

Leading by Example

Now, lifelong learning might seem like just a professional growth objective, but it's so much bigger than that. What example are you setting for your team, your company, and even the entire industry? Staying ahead of industry trends. Fostering a culture where continuous improvement becomes the norm. By constantly learning, you're not just improving yourself—you're elevating your team's performance and making sure your organization stays competitive. Your team members and your peers look up to you. Denise Lee Yeh captures this perfectly: "No matter where you are in your career, the willingness to learn shows your team that you're not just their boss—you're their partner in growth." By learning alongside their teams, leaders foster trust, collaboration, and a culture of innovation.[18]

Some of the most valuable insights often emerge from collaborative conversations that challenge perspectives and spark fresh thinking. Consider introducing a "Learn and Share" initiative within your team—where colleagues briefly present insights from a recent course, industry event, or book. Or perhaps you could organize a "learning lunch," where one person presents an interesting concept or tool they've discovered, sparking a lively discussion.

Another simple yet effective approach is creating a dedicated "Learning and Growth" channel in your team chat. Here, everyone can share intriguing articles, inspiring podcasts, or actionable insights they've picked up. It's an easy way to keep the conversation around learning alive and to inspire curiosity in others. This broadens collective knowledge but also strengthens team connections and shared goals.

As a leader, you define the culture and vision of your organization. But your influence extends beyond your company—you set the standard for the entire industry, inspiring innovation and change at a much larger scale. Imagine that. At the end of the day, nurturing resilience, embracing lifelong learning, and harnessing the power of grit are all interconnected. They feed into each other, creating a cycle of growth that's both challenging and incredibly rewarding.

At the heart of resilience, grit, and lifelong learning lies a simple but powerful truth: growth is a choice. It's both the decision and determination to show up, to rise after setbacks, and to keep exploring new paths to adapt and succeed.

What was the popular phrase "Lord, give me coffee to change the things I can, and wine to accept the things I can't."? Jokes aside, if I could leave with one message it would be this: be bold enough to fail, brave enough to keep going, and wise enough to keep learning.

- **Resilient Leadership:** The more senior your role in a company, the higher your resilience is likely to be. For example: 37% of upper management are highly resilient.[19] How can you leverage your leadership position to model resilience and support others in developing their ability to adapt and thrive?
- **Purpose Fuels Grit:** Leaders who deeply care about their mission are better equipped to overcome obstacles and sustain effort. What is a long-term goal that ignites your passion? How can you cultivate perseverance to pursue it despite challenges along the way?
- **Failing Forward:** Reframe failure as a stepping stone. How can you turn a recent setback into a learning opportunity? What valuable lessons did it teach you that success could not?
- **Stay Curious:** Successful leaders remain learners. Which new industry trend or tool will you tackle this month, and how can it give you a competitive edge?
- **Master Change:** Leaders who continually learn are best equipped for change. What trend or innovation will you explore next to future-proof your leadership?
- **Unlearn to Relearn:** Unlearning outdated practices is as important as acquiring new ones. What is one belief or habit you're ready to let go of to make space for better strategies?

9 | Work-Life Integration in a High-Powered Career

We don't have to do all of it alone. We were never meant to.

—Brené Brown[1]

Have you ever noticed how men are rarely asked about balancing work and life? Yet for women, it's a question that seems to follow us everywhere. It's almost like work-life "balance" has become something only we've signed up for, a women's issue to solve. Instead of striving for this elusive equilibrium, what if we focused on integration? How can we blend work, family, personal time, and rest into a life that feels authentic and fulfilling?

Too often, *work-life integration* becomes just a fancy term that still prioritizes work over life. If we want women to truly thrive, the narrative needs to change—life needs to come first. Stephanie Domas, a mother of four and Chief Information Security Officer at Canonical,[2] offers a refreshingly honest approach to managing a demanding career with family life.

She emphasizes the importance of being intentional with time: "For me, that means sometimes putting family before work, and knowing when to make that call," she says.

I've learned that when we try to do everything perfectly, we end up feeling overworked, overwhelmed, and overloaded. Burnout is not a badge of honor. It means we need a break—a real one—to reset our physical, mental, and emotional state. We can't do our best when we're constantly running on empty.

I've been on this journey myself—as a mother, a CEO, and the leader of a global network of 150,000 members. I've realized it's less about juggling separate pieces and more about weaving them together. Whether it's caring for a newborn, supporting an aging parent, or managing other responsibilities, we need to create a life where all these pieces can coexist. Flexibility was and still is a game-changer for me and many other women.

Gen Z might be onto something here. They're not looking for balance; they're redefining success altogether.[3] For them, work is just one part of life—not something that should overshadow everything else. Maybe we can learn from that perspective.

Work-life balance suggests a perfect split between work and personal life, which rarely matches reality. Integration accepts that these areas overlap—and that's okay. The goal isn't to keep them separate but to blend them in a way that allows us to thrive in both.

To illustrate the difference between work-life balance and work-life integration, let's compare the two approaches (Table 9.1).

Table 9.1   Key Differences Between Work-Life Balance and Work-Life Integration

	Work-Life Balance	**Work-Life Integration**
Definition	Equal separation between work and personal life.	Blending work and personal life to complement each other.
Approach	Clear boundaries keep work and personal time separate.	Flexibility allows activities to intermingle as needed.

	Work-Life Balance	Work-Life Integration
Goal	Achieve an even split of time and energy between work and life.	Create synergy where work and life enhance one another.
Mindset	Views work and life as competing priorities needing balance.	Sees work and life as complementary parts of a fulfilling whole.
Time Management	Fixed schedules with strict separation; minimal overlap.	Flexible schedules adapting to personal and professional needs.
Risks	• Guilt if perfect balance isn't achieved. • Rigidity may cause missed opportunities.	• Blurred boundaries can lead to overworking. • Potential burnout without limits.
Examples	• Leaving work at the same time daily. • Not checking emails after hours.	• Taking personal calls during work. • Adjusting work hours for family events.
Ideal For	Those who prefer clear boundaries and structure.	Individuals thriving on flexibility and a holistic approach.

Understanding the difference between balance and integration is the first step. Now, let's dive into five intentional strategies that have helped me—and can hopefully help you—effectively integrate work and life in a way that feels authentic and sustainable.

Five Strategies for Effective Work–Life Integration

Over the years, wearing multiple hats has taught me valuable lessons. Here are five intentional strategies that have made a real difference for me:

1. Plan, schedule, and create systems.
2. Focus on high-impact activities and money-generating tasks.
3. Delegate, Automate, Empower (DAE).

4. Build and grow your support network.

5. Dedicate time to recharge (especially when things get tough).

Plan, Schedule, and Create Systems

Effective planning and scheduling are essential when you're managing multiple responsibilities. My golden rule? I always schedule the important personal stuff first—family celebrations, my daughter's school events, doctor's appointments. If I don't block out that time and set reminders, work has a way of creeping into every available space.

Whether you're managing a team, a company, or personal commitments, a well-thought-out plan helps you stay on top of everything. Build systems that streamline your workflow, making it easier to stay organized and focused. Planning involves more than scheduling meetings; it includes creating repeatable processes that save time, reduce decision fatigue, and free up mental space for big-picture tasks.

For example, every Sunday evening, I sit down with a cup of tea and map out my week. I reserve time for events like my daughter's ballet recital. I also block every Monday morning from 9 to 10 a.m. for "thinking time"—dedicated solely to strategic planning.

Of course, obstacles can arise; unexpected work demands pop up despite our best efforts. In those moments, I try to be flexible but firm in protecting my personal commitments. Communicating clearly with my team and colleagues about my availability is key.

Consider integrating your calendar with your task management system, so everything flows seamlessly. Tools like Make.com and Zapier can be extremely helpful. Block out time for focused work, family, and even downtime. Treat your schedule like an investment—every block of time should serve a purpose.

As they say, "What gets scheduled, gets done."

Focus on High-Impact Activities and Money-Generating Tasks

Prioritizing tasks that truly make a difference—those that drive impact and revenue—is essential. This is how you demonstrate your value and get noticed for the right reasons by aligning with promotable tasks.

Early in my career, I was the go-to person for everything—organizing team lunches, taking meeting notes, you name it. While being helpful felt good, I realized these tasks weren't propelling my career forward. I shifted my focus to projects that showcased my leadership and strategic thinking, like spearheading a new product launch.

Making this shift wasn't without challenges. Saying "no" to tasks can feel uncomfortable. I remember worrying about disappointing colleagues or being seen as uncooperative. However, I realized that every time I said "yes" to something that didn't align with my priorities, I was essentially saying "no" to something more important.

To overcome this, I began practicing the art of polite refusal. Instead of a blunt "no," I'd say, "I appreciate you thinking of me, but I'm currently focusing on a project that requires my full attention." This approach allowed me to maintain professional relationships while staying true to my goals.

I started regularly assessing my tasks by asking, "Does this activity significantly contribute to my goals or the company's objectives?" If the answer was no, I'd consider delegating, automating, postponing or dropping it. This habit became a powerful tool in managing my time and energy.

A practical tip that helped me was leveraging tools like the Eisenhower Matrix[4] to prioritize tasks based on urgency and importance. It guided me to focus on what truly mattered and let go of what didn't.

If you're unsure about which tasks are high-impact, it might help to have a conversation with your manager or mentor. Understanding how your work contributes to the company's goals will help you prioritize effectively. Discussing my career aspirations with my mentor opened doors to opportunities aligned with my strengths and interests.

Remember, focusing your energy on activities that showcase your leadership and strategic thinking not only advances your career but also adds significant value to your organization. Work smarter, not harder.

Delegate, Automate, Empower (DAE)

Embrace the idea that while you can do anything, you can't do everything. Freeing yourself from non-strategic tasks by delegating, automating, and empowering your team allows you to focus on what truly matters.

Delegate   The moment I realized that some tasks didn't require my personal touch and could be handled by others just as effectively, if not better, I started delegating. For instance, when I asked a team member to take over managing our organization's social media posts, this freed up my time and provided an opportunity for them to develop new skills.

Delegating wasn't without challenges. Initially, I worried about losing control or that tasks wouldn't be completed to my standards. Overcoming this involved building trust and providing clear instructions. Regular check-ins helped ease my concerns and ensured everything stayed on track.

Having the right personal assistant can revolutionize the way you work. By handling tasks like scheduling and managing emails, they free you to focus on leadership and innovation. However, the key lies in finding the right fit—an ill-suited assistant can add stress rather than ease it.

Start by identifying the tasks you need help with and look for someone experienced in those areas. Equally important is ensuring compatibility in working styles and values, as a good match fosters seamless collaboration. Clear expectations are essential from the outset, along with maintaining open communication to build a partnership based on trust and feedback. With the right assistant, you'll enhance your productivity and create a supportive dynamic that drives success.

Automate In the era of AI, not automating routine tasks feels like a missed opportunity. There are many tools designed to make our lives easier. For me, automating repetitive tasks was a game-changer.

I used to spend significant time sorting and responding to routine emails. Then I discovered tools like Make.com combined with ChatGPT/OpenAI that could filter messages using advanced rules and even suggest automated responses. Scheduling tools like Calendly eliminated the back-and-forth of setting up meetings. I started using project management platforms like Monday.com to automate task assignments and deadlines.

Initially, I was hesitant to rely on automation, fearing it might seem impersonal. However, I realized that automating routine tasks allowed me to dedicate more time and energy to areas where a personal touch truly mattered.

Empower Set your team up for success by creating clear processes and structures. Provide them with the vision and autonomy they need to make decisions and own their tasks. Empowered teams can take initiatives off your plate, enabling you to lead more effectively.

Stephanie Domas empowers her team by normalizing open discussions about family life in the workplace: "I used to see people trying to hide that they were leaving early to pick up a sick kid. I didn't want that culture for my team. I talk openly about my family so others feel comfortable doing the same."

Build and Grow Your Support Network

Cultivating a support network of family, friends, and colleagues can make a world of difference during challenging times. In my journey, I've leaned on my support network whenever possible. For instance, when I was preparing for a major conference while our daughter was recovering from an illness, my partner's brother unexpectedly stepped in to help. We hadn't expected him to be available, but we asked, and he offered his support without hesitation. Knowing our child was being cared for allowed me to focus fully on my professional responsibilities.

Reeny Sondhi, Chief Digital Officer at Twilio,[5] shared how her support systems have been instrumental throughout her career. "My husband, who's a senior executive himself, has always had my back, and we co-parent without the stereotypical 'mom does this, dad does that' mindset. We step in for each other, whether it's at home or work. Having that kind of relationship has been key to my success."

She also emphasized the importance of friends: "It's not just about the immediate family. Having friends who are there for you, especially when you're balancing so much, is incredibly important. They offer a different kind of support—whether it's lending a listening ear or helping out in a pinch."

Jennie Baird, Chief Product Officer at BBC Studios, shared: "When my child was little, my mom would arrive at my place every morning at 6:15 so I could get to work by 7 a.m. I also relied on the help of a nanny, an evening nanny, and a weekend nanny. I couldn't have managed it all without my amazing support network." She further added, "It's striking how often men have it easier in these situations—they frequently have a stay-at-home wife managing everything at home, allowing them to focus entirely on their careers without the same level of juggling."

Having a strong network at work is just as important, as mentioned in Chapter 4. When things get tough, having colleagues, mentors, and professional connections who understand your challenges and can provide guidance makes all the difference.

Dedicate Time to Recharge (Especially When Things Get Tough)

In a culture that celebrates constant hustle, it can feel like rest is a luxury rather than a necessity. But here's the truth: if you don't take time to rest, your body will force you to. I've fallen into this trap more times than I'd like to admit.

For me, traveling is one of the best ways to recharge. And I don't mean work trips where you're stuck in the airport-plane-taxi-hotel-conference-airport-home routine. I mean real travel—exploring a country I've never been to before. It's my way of hitting the reset button. Every time, I learn something new about the world and myself. Plus, it helps me refocus and come back more energized.

Take, for example, a trip I took to Malta with a close friend while working on the book. Sure, I got sick at first (as life goes), but once I recovered, I knocked out two chapters in just a week! Normally, it takes me anywhere from one to three weeks to finish a chapter, depending on other responsibilities—work meetings, deadlines, vacations, medical appointments—you name it.

Other leaders share similar experiences. Reeny Sondhi highlights the importance of carving out time for herself, even with her busy schedule as a tech leader and mother of twins. She told me, "I take time to recharge. Whether it's something small, like getting a massage or meditating for 15 minutes before bed—these moments help me relax and sleep better. When I don't do it, I feel the difference."

Similarly, Janet Robertson, Global CIO at RS Group,[6] stresses the importance of completely disconnecting: "When I go diving, it's my true escape. No phones, no emails—just me and the ocean. It's my way to recharge, and the more stressful the year, the more time I spend under water."

You might think, "I don't have time to rest," or feel guilty about taking time for yourself. I used to feel that way too. Then I realized that neglecting rest affects my well-being and reduces my effectiveness in both personal and professional spheres.

Another obstacle is the fear of appearing less dedicated at work. But setting boundaries is crucial. Domas emphasizes the importance of setting clear boundaries between work and personal time—especially after hours. She shared, "I don't respond to work emails after hours unless it's an urgent matter. I want my team to know that it's okay to unplug and focus on family during those times."[7]

Scheduling rest is essential. Literally blocking off time on your calendar to "rest" or "recharge" and treating it like any other important appointment can make a huge difference. If a weekend getaway isn't feasible, starting with small acts of self-care—a 15-minute walk, reading a book, or practicing mindfulness—can be incredibly rejuvenating.

You Can Have It All, but Maybe Not All at Once

Work-life integration involves making tough choices. You might miss your child's recital due to a critical board meeting or pass on a major conference to care for an elderly parent. It's easy to feel guilty when you can't be everywhere at once, but that doesn't mean you're failing.

Reflect on how far you've come. Maybe you were the first in your family to attend college or reached a leadership role as an immigrant in a male-dominated industry. Don't let one missed event diminish your accomplishments—you've earned your place at the table.

Research[8] shows that women spend nearly three times more per day on household and childcare duties than men. The issue isn't that we're not working hard enough; it's that workplaces haven't adapted to support us.

According to the Women in the Workplace 2024 report,[9] "Regardless of seniority at work, women continue to do more at home." Senior-level women are more than four times more likely than men to handle most or all household responsibilities—35% compared to just 8% of men. This unequal distribution adds to the mental load we carry alongside our professional duties, increasing pressure to "manage it all."

Flexibility Is Everything

For decades, workplaces forced women to choose between career and family. But women didn't need to make a binary choice; the system needed to change. Some companies still demand rigid office hours, as if it's 1995. Flexibility is more than clocking hours; it requires trust in employees' ability to manage their time effectively.

The Women in the Workplace 2024 report further states, "Flexibility is especially important to women, who report having more focused time to get their work done when working remotely."[10] This flexibility helps us manage personal responsibilities alongside demanding work schedules.

However, not everyone feels empowered to utilize flexible options. A senior executive confided in me: "I used to go into the office five days a week, no matter what. My commute was one hour and forty minutes one way, but I felt like I had to show my face, especially when my team was growing. Even though most people worked from home on Fridays, I felt obligated to be in the office to set the right example."

Looking back, she reflects on missed opportunities to prioritize family: "I could have wrapped up meetings by 4 p.m. and attended my daughter's concert, but I didn't. I stayed at work, even when I didn't need to."

Her story highlights the internal and external pressure on women in leadership to be present at work, sometimes at the expense of personal moments. Flexibility includes feeling empowered to set boundaries that support both your career and your personal life.

When a company hires you, they should trust your expertise and ability to get the job done on your terms. Whether you're at home between Zoom meetings, dropping your kids off at daycare, fitting in a workout, or prepping dinner after 6 p.m., what matters is your output, not your physical presence. Success isn't measured by being chained to a desk but by achieving results.

A viral TikTok video by Brielle Asero, a young professional, highlighted frustration with the 9-to-5 grind and a long commute. She shared, "If it was remote, you log off at 5 and you're home and everything's fine."[11] Her words resonated with many, shedding light on how rigid work schedules can limit personal time.

Not everyone feels the same about remote work. Padmaja Dasari, CIO at Nextdoor,[12] offers a contrasting view: "I hate working from home," she says. "Being a woman, I find it distracting. At the office, I can completely focus on work. But at home, I see the clutter, the unfinished chores, and it pulls me out of my work. Men don't seem to notice these things the way we [women] do."

Dasari's experience underscores the complexity of the work-from-home dynamic for women who often manage both household and office tasks. Flexibility means having the choice to select what works best for you—be it working from the office, home, or a hybrid model. Hybrid work could be a solution, allowing employees to choose when they need to be in the office for collaborative activities while offering remote work when it fits their lifestyle.

When to Say "No"

Saying "no" is essential in managing your time and energy. If it doesn't excite you or align with your goals, it's a no.

One practical area to apply this is in meetings. Do you know how much time and money are wasted in long, unproductive meetings? There's a study[13] that revealed more than $299 billion is spent annually in the US on such meetings. Let's face it—we've all been in meetings that could have been an email. Being intentional with our time is crucial. Shorter, focused meetings respect everyone's schedule and boost productivity. When meetings are necessary, having a clear agenda helps.

"No" is a complete sentence. You don't owe an explanation to anyone (okay, except perhaps your manager). Embracing this changed my perspective:

- Say "no" to the meeting you don't need to attend.
- Say "no" to the job that no longer fulfills you.
- Say "no" to non-promotional work (and remember the earlier points about delegating and automating).
- Say "no" to tasks that AI can handle for you.

Every time you say "no" to something misaligned with your goals, you make space for things that do align. Protect your time and energy by using "no" as a tool for focus and clarity.

When to Say "Yes"

Embrace what truly lights you up. Say "yes" to opportunities that align with your values and bring you joy:

- Say "yes" to stepping on stage to speak at a conference—because why not you?
- Say "yes" to a special trip to Europe—where you can stroll through the streets of Rome, enjoy delicious gelato, and toast to life with

perfectly chilled prosecco. You've worked incredibly hard, and you deserve experiences that let you fully recharge and see the world.

- Say "yes" to the simple joy of a Disneyland trip with your child.
- Say "yes" to an essential career break—whether to take care of your mental health, travel, or finally do the things you've postponed for far too long.
- Say "yes" to the things that scare you because they're often the ones that will stretch you in incredible ways.
- Say "yes" to your dream job when it comes knocking.
- Say "yes" to opportunities that let you shine—whether it's being featured in an article or stepping into that next big role.

Most importantly, say "yes" to taking care of your physical, mental, and spiritual health. Block off time for yourself and treat it as non-negotiable—a standing meeting with your most important investor: you.

Motherhood Guilt

For many working mothers, the feeling of guilt can be draining—a constant conflict between being present for our children and pursuing professional ambitions. Society often expects mothers to be always available at home while excelling at work—a no-win situation.

Consider how fathers and mothers are perceived differently when prioritizing family. When a dad attends his child's event, he's praised as a "great dad." When a mom does the same, she risks being labeled "not committed enough" to her job. This double standard forces many women into an impossible juggling act, making us feel like we're failing on both fronts.

I interviewed Aysha Khan, CISO and CIO at Treasure Data.[14] As a mother of two, she emphasizes intentionality and open communication with her children. She explains, "I have two girls, and I approach my career and family with discipline and structure. I don't go on guilt trips. When I miss school events because of important meetings, I'm honest with them. I tell them, 'Mama has important work, and if I'm not there, it's because I'm out there making an impact.' And I expect the same from them as they grow—creating impact, making a difference."

Sandy Carter, COO at Unstoppable Domains,[15] shared her struggle with motherhood guilt. Early on, she missed important school events until another mom advised her: "Volunteer to manage the class calendar, so you'll always know when events are coming up."

Doomed If You Do, Doomed If You Don't

Whether you're a working mom or a working woman, sometimes it feels like you just can't win. The bias is real and exhausting.

For mothers, biases come as comments suggesting they're less committed to their careers—the "motherhood penalty." Questions like, "Is she going to need more time off with the kids?" or "Can she handle that big project with so much going on at home?" imply that having a family affects capability.

For women without children, assumptions often swing in the opposite direction: "She's probably too focused on her career to want a family," or "Why doesn't she have kids?" Such comments perpetuate the idea that without motherhood, a woman should easily handle long hours and extra responsibilities. Do you hear men being asked such questions? Whether childless by choice or circumstance, women are often unfairly labeled as cold, overly ambitious, or seen as deviating from traditional expectations. Remarks like, "She must have all the time in the world since she doesn't have kids," or worse, "She needs less money because she doesn't have children," reflect biases that devalue her time, contributions, and worth.

We need to recognize that every woman's life is different. Work-life integration should allow individuals to thrive, whether they're attending a child's soccer practice or going to a yoga class after work. Judgment only reinforces outdated views; it's time corporate culture caught up with reality.

Choose Your Partner Wisely

Corporate culture isn't the only place to discuss support; having a supportive partner can make all the difference.

As Sheryl Sandberg wisely said in *Lean In*, "The most important career decision you'll make is who you choose to marry."[16] It may sound bold, but your partner's support is critical to your success, both at work and in life.

Choosing a supportive partner has been one of the most impactful decisions of my life. Without my husband's encouragement and understanding, pursuing my career while raising our child would have been much harder. When work demanded late nights or travel, he stepped in—handling bedtime stories, school drop-offs, and everything in between.

This support forms the foundation of a strong relationship. It's not always easy—it requires communication, flexibility, and empathy—but it's essential for thriving both professionally and personally. Having someone who believes in you and is willing to share the journey makes all the difference.

Sandy Carter shares a similar view. She and her husband don't divide household tasks into "yours" and "mine"—they tackle everything together. This partnership allows both to thrive in their careers without feeling forced to choose between work and family. Such support empowers individuals, especially women, to succeed in all aspects of life.

As you reflect on your journey toward work-life integration, consider the choices that will help you create a fulfilling and sustainable life. Remember, it's not about striving for perfection; it's about making intentional decisions that align with your values and priorities.

- **Energy Over Time:** Great leaders prioritize their energy, not just their time. How can you optimize your physical, emotional, and mental energy to lead with clarity and impact, even in high-pressure situations?
- **Get Quality Sleep:** Research shows that sleep deprivation negatively impacts memory, decision-making, and emotional regulation. How can you prioritize better sleep to break free from the cycle of living on the edge of burnout?
- **Own Your Day:** Intentional planning empowers leaders to balance priorities and protect what matters most. Start by scheduling "Me Time" first—prioritize your well-being before adding work commitments. How can you reshape your day to align with your goals and create a sustainable rhythm?

- **Celebrate Imperfection:** Perfection is overrated. Embrace the freedom of letting go and focusing on progress over perfection. Accept that you can't do it all, and that's perfectly okay. What's one area of your life where you can trade self-criticism for self-compassion?
- **Guardrails for Growth:** Non-negotiable boundaries aren't walls; they're your pathway to thriving. What matters most to you, and how can you protect it while staying focused on your goals?
- **Success, Your Way:** The most powerful success stories are the ones you write yourself. Ditch the rulebook, redefine success on your own terms, and create a life that feels as good as it looks. What would that look like for you?

10

Joining Boards, Making an Impact, and Leaving a Legacy

The world is starving for new ideas and great leaders who will champion those ideas.

—Dr. Lisa Su, Chair and CEO at AMD[1]

You've made it. You're a Chief in Tech. So, time to give back to the community, right? The belief that giving back begins only once you've "arrived" is outdated. I see it differently: giving back should be part of our professional journey from the very beginning. A fancy title isn't a prerequisite for making a difference. Impact isn't measured by years of experience but by the value you provide to others, the mentorship and sponsorship you offer, and the knowledge you share.

Yes, a title can open doors, but every individual has the potential to make an impact—regardless of position or seniority. I remember when people laughed at me for calling myself a CEO in my mid-twenties. If I'd listened to those who doubted me—thinking I was too young or inexperienced—I wouldn't have become the leader I am today and

I probably wouldn't have been able to build a community of 150,000 members in such a relatively short time. I believe in learning by doing, not overthinking or waiting years to do something impactful.

Leaders give back not because it looks good or because they have resources like time and money—though these matter—but because of a deeper purpose. This purpose isn't about checking off a corporate responsibility box; it's rooted in a genuine commitment to see change reflected in your team, organization, and ultimately, the entire industry. We can't change the system for women in tech overnight; but we, women and allies, can do our part.

Reflecting on my journey so far, I'm truly grateful for the time, wisdom, and knowledge that impact-driven global tech leaders (including the leaders in this book) have generously given back to our own WomenTech Network community. The community needs it. With global organizations like Girls in Tech and Women Who Code shutting down, this support is absolutely crucial.

So, let's say you have enough years of experience, time, and financial resources to shake things up—to rewire, disrupt, reinvent yourself, try something new, solve problems, or help other visionary leaders do the same. There are a few things you might want to try: join a board (nonprofit, private, public, or advisory), become a founder, invest in startups (tech for good, impact investing), among many other ways to give back and leave a legacy.

Getting on Boards

Now, imagine this: you're sitting in a boardroom, surrounded by some of the biggest names in the industry. You're helping to shape the future of an entire company—not just as an executive, but as a board member. Sounds thrilling, doesn't it? But how do you actually get there?

Getting on a board can feel like breaking into a secret club. Success comes from building credibility (personal branding), gaining experience (starting with smaller boards or nonprofit roles), and expanding your network (connecting with existing board members and industry leaders).

Asha Keddy, former Corporate VP at Intel,[2] mentioned that landing a board position often feels like infiltrating a tight-knit circle: "Typically, it takes two to three years to get on a board, and even then, the process is about governance, not execution. Boards are traditionally made up of former CEOs, finance experts, and venture capitalists—people with specific connections.

You have to know people already on boards, and they often refer others when they're overcommitted themselves. It's all about expanding your network and letting your goals be known."

Betsy Atkins,[3] a boardroom legend who has served on more than 34 boards and been through 13 IPOs, advises building a board portfolio by starting with nonprofit boards, then private ones, and eventually moving to public boards: "If you think that you can really help a business, you can start small—start with private small boards and get experience. A lot of times, people start in the not-for-profit world and then go to smaller private boards." She adds, "It's unlikely if you've never done anything related at all that American Express or Google is going to tap you on the shoulder.... You have to kind of build up your portfolio."

There are several ways to approach board service, but in my view, four are the most relevant for you as a tech leader. They are with nonprofit boards, advisory boards, private company boards, and public company boards (Table 10.1).

Table 10.1   Types of Boards and Examples

Type of Board	Company Example	Women on Board	Potential Focus
Nonprofit Board	Girls Who Code	Carol Juel (EVP & CTO, Synchrony Financial)[a]	Supports strategic decisions aligning with the nonprofit's mission to close the gender gap in tech education.
	Code.org	Aileen Tang (Former Google Product Leader)[b]	Brings expertise in product leadership to expand access to computer science education, particularly for underrepresented students.

(continued)

Table 10.1   (*Continued*)

Type of Board	Company Example	Women on Board	Potential Focus
	AnitaB.org	Rebecca Parsons (Emerita CTO, Thoughtworks)[c]	Focuses on challenges faced by women and nonbinary individuals in tech, advancing diversity and inclusion.
Advisory Board	Microsoft Global Community Initiative	Jennifer Mason (Vice President Workforce Transformation & Learning, Planet Technologies)[d]	Provides strategic guidance, supports events, develops resources, and enhances platform engagement.
	HubSpot	Dr. Claudia Igbrude (Learning Technology Business Partner, PayPal)[e]	Advises on customer experience technologies and digital learning strategies.
Private Company Board	Databricks	Elena Donio (Former CEO, Axiom)[f]	Provides strategic direction in cloud innovation and talent strategy. Also serves on Benchling board.[g]

Type of Board	Company Example	Women on Board	Potential Focus
	Automattic	Sue Decker (CEO and Founder of Raftr)[h]	Provides strategic guidance in scaling global platforms and leveraging innovative technologies for community building and content management. Also serves on Chime Board.[i]
Public Company Board	Apple Inc. (AAPL)	Dr. Wanda Austin (Former CEO of The Aerospace Corporation)[j]	Provides strategic direction in technology innovation, and corporate governance.
	JPMorgan Chase (JPM)	Ginni Rometty (Former CEO of IBM)[k]	Focuses on governance, digital transformation, and AI integration.

(*continued*)

Table 10.1 (*Continued*)

Type of Board	Company Example	Women on Board	Potential Focus
	Shopify (SHOP)	Fidji Simo (CEO & Chair of Instacart)[l]	Provides leadership in digital transformation, AI, and e-commerce. Also serves on OpenAI's board.[m]

Note: These examples are illustrative. Please verify current board memberships as they may have changed.

[a]Code, Girls Who. 2024. "Our Team." Girls Who Code. November 4, 2024. https://girlswhocode.com/about-us/team.

[b]"Ladership." n.d. Code.Org. https://code.org/about/leadership.

[c]"The AnitaB.org Global Board of Trustees | AnitaB.org." 2024. AnitaB.Org. July1, 2024. https://anitab.org/our-team/board-of-trustees/.

[d]https://adoption.microsoft.com/en-us/microsoft-global-community-initiative/advisors/

[e]HubSpot. n.d. "HubSpot Advisory Board." https://www.hubspot.com/company/advisory-board.

[f]https://www.databricks.com/company/board-of-directors

[g]https://www.benchling.com/news/benchling-expands-executive-team-and-board-of-directors

[h]https://automattic.com/board/

[i]https://theorg.com/org/chime/org-chart/sue-decker

[j]Apple. n.d. "Apple Leadership." https://www.apple.com/leadership/.

[k]"Virginia M. Rometty." n.d. https://www.jpmorganchase.com/about/leadership/virginia-rometty.

[l]Shopify. "Board of Directors." *Shopify Investors*. Accessed November 19, 2024. https://shopifyinvestors.com/Governance/Board-of-Directors/default.aspx.

[m]Wikipedia contributors. 2024. "OpenAI." Wikipedia. November 15, 2024. https://en.wikipedia.org/wiki/OpenAI.

Nonprofit Boards

Organizations like Girls Who Code, Code.org, and AnitaB.org are making significant impacts in the tech industry. While these specific organizations might not have current board openings, you can look for smaller local nonprofits in your local community, city, state, or country; they don't have to be global or widely known. Beyond contributing to meaningful causes, serving on a nonprofit board helps you gain valuable governance and leadership experience. Nonprofits are increasingly seeking tech leaders to drive their digital strategies and expand their missions, such as promoting STEM education or advancing digital learning platforms. It could also be a non-tech or non-STEM-related cause that is dear to your heart. The key is to find an organization where you can make a difference.

Advisory Boards

Advisory boards are where the fun really begins. Often found in the fast-paced, high-energy world of startups or growth-stage companies, these boards are looking for one thing: your expertise. As an advisor, you can shape key decisions around product development, go-to-market strategies, or innovative tech solutions. While advisory board roles offer more flexibility than formal board positions, they still come with advisory agreements, meaning your guidance has real weight.

But advisory boards aren't limited to startups. Many large companies, such as Amazon, Google, Microsoft, and Salesforce, also have advisory boards that focus on specific topics or regions. These boards address critical areas like sustainability, AI ethics, and product innovation.

Boards can also be regional, addressing localized challenges and opportunities, or focused on specific industries or initiatives. Microsoft's Global Community Initiative Advisory Board, for example, collaborates on enhancing community experiences worldwide.

I've advised more than 20 startups over the course of several years, and what I've learned is that it's a mutually beneficial relationship—they get the benefit of my experience, and I gain insight into emerging technologies and business models. It's a fantastic way to stay on the cutting edge of industry trends while contributing to the success of emerging companies.

It's also a great opportunity to build relationships, gain insights, and position yourself. Plus, it's less of a time commitment, which can be helpful if you're balancing other responsibilities. For me, serving on advisory boards has allowed me to expand my network, learn from passionate entrepreneurs, and even discover new opportunities I wouldn't have encountered otherwise.

Private Company Boards

Private company boards are where things get serious. These companies might not be in the spotlight yet, but they're on the cusp of scaling big time—think tech-driven businesses backed by venture capital or family-owned enterprises gearing up for rapid growth. As a tech leader, your expertise in scaling operations, managing finances, and driving innovation is exactly what these boards are seeking.

And yes, there's often compensation involved—sometimes in the form of equity, sometimes as cash, or even a mix of both—depending on the company's stage and resources. Early-stage startups may primarily offer equity, tying your success directly to theirs, while larger private companies or venture-backed firms often provide a combination of cash retainers and equity grants. This is your chance to apply your governance knowledge while steering a company toward its next big breakthrough. Imagine being part of a fintech or cybersecurity company's journey as they scale—this is where your expertise truly moves the needle.

Take Stripe, for example, a global payment powerhouse, or Databricks, a leader in data and AI innovation. Their boards bring together founders, venture capital representatives, and industry experts to guide them through exponential growth and prepare for potential future milestones like IPOs.

Throughout my time advising startups, I've had the privilege of contributing my expertise to innovative companies while earning equity in many of them. Seeing these companies succeed has been both professionally fulfilling and financially rewarding—a true win-win.

Public Company Boards

Landing a seat on a public company board? Now we're talking top-tier responsibility, impact, and prestige. Whether it's with giants like Apple,

Microsoft, or Nvidia—or innovators like Airbnb, Netflix, or Spotify—this is where leadership is tested on a whole new level. Public boards oversee some of the biggest players in tech, and with that comes high-stakes fiduciary duties, shareholder relations, and governance challenges that can make or break a company's future.

The good news? Tech expertise is in high demand, especially when it comes to navigating digital transformations, mergers and acquisitions, and the ever-evolving cybersecurity landscape. The challenge? These seats are highly competitive, and it's not just about what you know—it's about who you know. But if you're a leader who's been at the helm of innovation and have the vision to guide a company through today's complex digital world, then a public board seat is the pinnacle of influence.

One former C-level executive shared, "Even if they paid me millions, I wouldn't go back to my CIO role. No way. It's more fun to be on boards." This highlights how board service is a fulfilling way to make a high-level impact.

Whether it's a public, private, advisory or nonprofit board, there's an opportunity for you to make an impact—but first, you need to get on board. Literally.

Regardless of the type of board, you normally need to get recommended. This typically happens when you've built a strong reputation, positioned yourself as a board-ready leader in your field, and your skills align with the needs of the board. You've made yourself visible to executive search recruiters, your peers, your network, and have made strategic connections with experienced board members so people know about you. In this case, you're very likely to receive what many board members describe as "the call"—an invitation because of your expertise, industry presence, or a recommendation from a trusted network.

This of course should not stop you from proactively seeking out board opportunities by expressing interest, reaching out to existing board members or company leadership, and making a case for how your skills and insights would benefit the organization.

Four Steps to Get on a Company Board

Navigating your way onto a board can seem like cracking a secret code, but Daphne E. Jones, CEO at The Board Curators and former CIO at GE

HealthCare Global Services, and 3x Corporate Board Member[4], breaks it down into actionable steps:

#1 Know Your Superpower   "Know your superpower. Know yourself and know how to parlay that superpower into value." You need to understand the unique expertise you bring to the table and how it can directly benefit a company. Boards are looking for individuals whose skills align with their strategic goals. Whether it's cybersecurity, digital transformation, or financial strategy, identify your niche, and be ready to showcase how you can add value.

#2 Expand Your Network   "Getting new friends is the second thing that I say, and I kind of say it jokingly—you know the people around you, they're great for moral support. But unless they're already on a board, they're not going to help you get on a board." While your existing network might be supportive, you need to proactively build relationships with those who are already involved in board service. Attend industry events, join professional organizations, and don't hesitate to reach out to board members in your field. These individuals are more likely to refer you for opportunities because they're in the circles where board appointments are discussed.

#3 Position Yourself for the Right Boards   "If you know supply chain and that's your expertise, you should go after companies that might have supply chain challenges. Or, if you're a marketing guru, you go after companies that are dealing with customer experience issues." The key is to identify boards where your superpower is most needed. Research companies facing challenges that align with your expertise and position yourself accordingly. To strengthen your credibility, consider obtaining relevant certifications and joining organizations such as the NACD (National Association of Corporate Directors). These credentials demonstrate your commitment to governance excellence and make you a more attractive candidate for board roles. Additionally, tailor your board resume to highlight relevant experiences and be prepared to articulate how your skills can address their specific needs.

#4 Leverage Referrals   "You go after those people, find new people that are already on boards that may be on too many boards already. Because the next time they get a phone call about a board, they're going to say, 'I can't get on a board, but I know someone who's amazing.'" Building relationships with well-connected board members can lead to valuable referrals when they are overcommitted. When they receive opportunities they can't pursue, you might be the first person they recommend.

Monique Jeanne Morrow, a global technology leader and President and Co-founder at The Humanized Internet,[5] emphasized the significance of board diversity and the responsibility that comes with it. She said, "If you have composition on the board that reflects your society or reflects your company or your customers, then you've succeeded."[6] Diverse boards are not just a nice-to-have; they're a business imperative. They bring varied perspectives that can drive innovation, improve decision-making, and better represent the stakeholders a company serves.

Alignment and Passion

One executive at a large health tech company shared with me how she reached a point where her work no longer aligned with her deeper goals. "I wanted to give back and serve on boards that aligned with my passions, whether that was through paid roles, nonprofit work, or advisory positions. It felt like the next chapter." But there were restrictions. "They [her employer] said I couldn't join any board that had even a remote connection to healthcare. And that's where my passion lies. Even if it was an AI company with potential to enter healthcare in the future, it was a no-go."

Her experience highlights a common challenge: navigating corporate policies that limit outside engagements, especially when those opportunities align closely with your passions and expertise. It's essential to understand your company's policies and, if possible, negotiate terms that allow you to pursue meaningful board service without conflicts of interest.

Making an Impact

Your contributions can create waves of change in so many beautiful ways: by building ventures that harness technology to solve systemic challenges, mentoring future innovators, investing in purpose-driven startups, or using your network to advocate for equitable access to technology. Your skills, resources, and influence can drive meaningful change. You've climbed the corporate ladder, faced countless challenges, and demonstrated your leadership. Now, it's time to take those experiences and channel them into something of your own.

Starting Your Own Impact-Driven Venture

Whether it's launching a nonprofit, creating a consultancy, starting a venture fund, or championing a cause, the opportunities to drive change are vast. The key is to align your next venture with what you genuinely care about. Ask yourself: What issues resonate most deeply with me? What challenges am I uniquely equipped to solve? Many leaders find themselves drawn to causes that promote sustainability, mentorship, or innovation, but the most impactful ventures are those rooted in personal passion and purpose.

It starts with clarity. Define the scope of your project. What is your why? What problem would you be working to solve? Who will benefit? How will you measure success? For some, this could mean mentoring other leaders and sharing the wisdom you've gained. For others, it might be investing in underrepresented founders or developing a program to tackle a deeply personal challenge.

Execution is where ideas come to life. Ideas are everywhere, but it's your ability to take them from concept to action that sets you apart. Start small and validate. Pilot your ideas, seek feedback from trusted peers, and refine as you progress. Remember, don't fall in love with the solution—fall in love with the problem you're solving. While solutions can evolve, your consistent dedication to addressing the problem is what drives meaningful and lasting impact.

Take my own experience with WomenTech Network. What began as a straightforward idea—amplifying the voices of women in tech—grew into a global movement. It required us to pivot, adapt, and persist, but our mission always guided us. That clarity and resilience turned what started as a project into something impactful.

Fundraising

The challenges and biases women face in entrepreneurship are very real, and they mirror the ones women face in tech. According to a 2020 Pitch-Book study, female-founded startups received only about 2.3% of all venture capital investment in the US. This isn't because women aren't pitching innovative ideas, but because the venture capital world has historically been dominated by men. It's not necessarily always conscious bias, but there's a comfort in familiarity. Investors tend to bet on founders who feel familiar to them, who come from similar backgrounds, who think and act like them.

So what can we do about it? This means we have to break past that initial barrier of familiarity. We have to find the investors who are ready to step outside their comfort zones—those who are seeking diverse perspectives and fresh thinking. Investors need to recognize that a founder who doesn't look like them might just have the grit, vision, and capability to build something remarkable.

One seasoned executive I spoke with, who is now running a successful company, shared with me her fundraising challenges. She explained how, in 90% of her meetings, she was the only woman in the room and investors would often direct their questions to her male colleagues, despite the fact that she was leading the raise. Can you imagine the frustration? She emphasized the importance of finding investors who share your values and who see the long-term potential of your business, not just the immediate financials. She added: "It's like a marriage." You need to find investors who truly believe in what you're building and who align with your vision.

But here's the good news: Female-led venture capital firms are on the rise.[7] We're seeing more women supporting and investing in other women, and that's changing the game. I know they are still like unicorns but every bit of progress counts. Organizations like Female Founders Fund, All Raise, and Backstage Capital are paving the way for women entrepreneurs to thrive.

Impact Investing: Turning Capital into Change

What if you're ready for more than just building your own venture? What if you're thinking bigger—about how you can support others, solve large-scale problems, and leave a lasting legacy through the investments you make? Just like founders pour passion into their startups, you can leverage your resources to make a real impact on the world. This is where impact investing comes into play—where your money doesn't just work for financial returns but also drives meaningful change.

It's not just about multiplying your returns (though that's always nice); it's about investing in businesses designed to create both profit and purpose. As an impact investor, you're not only looking for companies that make a difference—you're seeking out ventures that tackle societal challenges head-on. Think climate change, poverty, inequality. And yes, you're expecting a solid financial return as well. It's the perfect alignment of doing good while doing well.

So, how do you start investing with purpose? First, ask yourself: What causes do you care about? Fighting against climate change? Expanding access to healthcare? What challenges have you faced, or what issues have you seen others struggle with? What would you want to improve for the next generation? Your "why" becomes your compass, guiding you toward investments that reflect your core values.

For example, maybe you're passionate about gender equality because you've experienced firsthand how hard it is to break barriers. Or perhaps you care deeply about climate action because you want to ensure a better future for generations to come. Whatever drives you, align your investments with that purpose. You have the power to direct your resources toward solving the problems that matter most to you.

To further ground your impact, you can look to the United Nations Sustainable Development Goals (SDGs). These goals offer a global framework to address pressing challenges, from ensuring quality education to promoting clean energy. By investing in the projects and companies that are aligned with SDGs, you ensure that your money is not only financially viable but also making the world a better place.[8]

And here's the exciting part: impact investing doesn't just transform the world—it can transform your investment portfolio, too. As more companies demonstrate that they can be both profitable and purpose-driven, impact investing is proving that doing good and achieving financial success can go hand in hand.

Once you've identified issues that ignite your passion, research funds or platforms that specialize in impact investing. Many funds focus on businesses aligned with gender equality, climate action, and healthcare.

Take inspiration from these female-led companies that are making waves:

Company	CEO/ Founder	Core Business	SDGs
Zoox	Aicha Evans	Redefining urban mobility with zero-emission vehicles	SDG 11: Sustainable Cities and Communities, SDG 13: Climate Action
Ellevest	Sallie Krawcheck	Focusing on financial empowerment for women	SDG 5: Gender Equality, SDG 8: Decent Work and Economic Growth
The Honest Company	Jessica Alba	Producing eco-friendly products	SDG 12: Responsible Consumption and Production, SDG 3: Good Health and Well-being

Note: These examples are illustrative of their alignment with the UN SDGs based on their missions and impact.

Whether through your investments, leadership, or the businesses you build, you have the opportunity to shape more than just financial returns—you can shape the future. What kind of world do you want to help create? What lasting impact do you want to leave behind for future generations, for women in tech, and for the industry as a whole?

That's when the real question comes into play: What legacy will you leave?

Building a Legacy

At some point in our careers, we stop focusing solely on immediate goals and start thinking about our legacy. What impact do you want to leave behind? How will your work shape the future for women in tech and the broader industry?

Building a legacy goes beyond personal success. It's about ensuring that the changes you implement, the barriers you break, and the opportunities you create became sustainable. Just like the women before us who paved the way—for us to work, vote, lead, run for office, become executives, start our own ventures, raise money, and invest—the list goes on. Your legacy might be tied to a specific innovation, a culture shift in your company, or the people you've mentored and supported along the way.

Consider how you can build a legacy that reflects your values. For some, this might mean pushing for more inclusive hiring practices. For others, it could involve launching a scholarship or creating programs that make tech more accessible to underrepresented groups. For me, it's about growing our WomenTech Network and Executive Women in Tech Network, organizing conferences to foster innovation and collaboration and facilitate meaningful conversations. What's your vision? How would you like to be remembered?

Leave People Better Than You Found Them

I remember seeing a quote on the wall of a coworking space years ago: "Leave people better than you found them." At the time, I pondered what that truly meant in the context of leadership. How do you "leave people better than you found them"?

As I write this final chapter, I'm reflecting on power, respect, and the lasting impact we have on others. What if the true measure of success isn't the title you hold or the power you wield, but how you leave the people around you? Real leadership shows up in the way you inspire others to believe in themselves, how you create opportunities for them to shine, and the energy you pour into building others up. It's less about holding the reins and more about opening the doors for others to walk through.

Once, I was invited to a very exclusive women's dinner hosted by a highly accomplished female tech leader. To say I was surprised would be an understatement. It had only been a couple of months since I started WomenTech Network, and I couldn't believe I was sitting among leaders who ran enterprise-level companies, held titles like CEO, CIO, and Managing Director, and were also investors and keynote speakers, including the ones you see on the *Forbes* covers. The sheer number of awards and the collective years of wisdom these women brought to the table were almost impossible to count.

At first, I felt completely out of place. Imposter syndrome crept in, and I couldn't shake the feeling that I didn't belong in such distinguished company. These women had accomplished so much, and I wondered what I could possibly contribute to the conversation.

Then the host turned to me and said, "Tell us about WomenTech Network. I've been hearing great things."

Her genuine curiosity and encouragement instantly shifted the atmosphere for me. She listened intently as I shared my journey, asked thoughtful questions, and even related it to her own experiences championing women in tech within her company. It wasn't just the validation—it was the way she made me feel seen, valued, and respected, despite the difference in our titles, years of experience and achievements.

That moment was transformative. It taught me something profound about leadership: it's not about being the most important person in the room. It's about creating space for others to shine, showing respect and encouragement, and uplifting those around you. Moreover, being in that circle of accomplished leaders showed me what great leadership looks like.

"Leaving people better than you found them" means empowering them when they doubt themselves. Promoting them when you see their potential. Encouraging them when they need that extra push. It's forgiving them when they make mistakes—because we all do. It's listening when they need to be heard and appreciating them when they've put in the hard work. These small moments define leadership.

Power, especially the kind that comes with a title, can be taken from you in an instant. It's fleeting, shifting with circumstances. But respect? That's different. Respect stays with you. Respect is the lasting currency of leadership. It's built on how you treat others and becomes the foundation of the legacy you leave behind. People won't remember the authority you had or the decisions you made from a place of power. What they will remember is how you made them feel—whether that was seen, valued, and uplifted.

To truly "leave people better than you found them" means focusing on human connection. It's about helping them find their strengths and giving them the space to grow. Showing up for them. Guiding them. Giving them the courage to stretch beyond what they thought was possible. The people you inspire, the doors you open, and the respect you cultivate—those are the things that really matter.

As I reflect on this, I realize that respect isn't something you can demand. It's something you earn. It comes from your character, your values, and how you show up—not just in the big moments, but in the small, everyday ones. In the end, the legacy of a great leader isn't measured by the power they held. It's measured by the positive change they fostered in the lives of others. That's how you leave people better than you found them.

Tech Needs More Leaders Like You

There are moments when the workplace feels overwhelmingly unfair. Times when it seems like no matter how hard you push, how much you achieve, you're met with resistance or, worse, indifference. You may find yourself questioning everything—your decisions, your path, even your place in tech. But let me tell you: you absolutely belong here. In fact, we need you now more than ever!

The tech world is calling out for leaders like you—leaders who aren't afraid to drive change, make an impact, and build a future where everyone belongs. Especially in times when technologies like generative AI are rapidly evolving, your voice is incredibly important.

Tech needs leaders like you. Leaders who will challenge the status quo, create sustainable change, and ensure that the innovations we build work for everyone, not just a select few. Imagine designing a smartphone that actually fits a woman's hand—something as simple as making technology more inclusive but so often overlooked. Imagine leading research that detects women's cancers earlier, using AI and data to save lives in ways we've never thought possible.

And it's beyond tech. It's about inspiring the next generation. We need you to be the role model for young girls who are curious about the tech world, who want to create, invent, and innovate but feel like they don't belong. You're the one who will show them that STEM isn't just a "boy's thing," that they can fall in love with technology, and that their ideas matter. We need leaders like you to support them, to lift them up when they doubt themselves—just like you might be doubting yourself now.

But don't stop there. We need bold leaders who are ready to break new ground, to shatter the silicon ceiling that has been intact for far too long.

We need more female CTOs, CIOs, CPOs, CMOs, CEOs, CDOs (invent your own C-level title!) leading major tech companies and high-growth startups—women who will influence the direction of technology at its core. We need women like you to start companies, bring innovations to life, and create work environments where diversity isn't just a checkbox but a core value. We need more women running for office, shaping policy, and advocating for change from the highest platforms. Because when women lead, the world changes for the better.

What if you set the standard for what inclusive, ethical, and groundbreaking leadership could look like?

There's still so much work to be done. Research[9] shows that when women are involved in leadership, organizations are more innovative, ethical, and profitable. But we're still underrepresented in areas that desperately need our voices. We need more women leading in AI, ensuring this transformative technology is developed with fairness, ethics, and empathy, avoiding biases that can perpetuate inequality. We need more women tackling climate tech, solving the most pressing environmental challenges of our time. We need women in healthcare tech, revolutionizing how we detect diseases, treat patients, and manage public health crises. And we need more women building cybersecurity systems that protect everyone, including the most vulnerable and ensure everyone's privacy and safety online. And beyond tech, we need more women in policy and politics, championing legislation that fosters equality, peace, and sustainable growth. Together, these are the powerful technologies and platforms that will define the future—and we can't afford to design them without you.

Yes, the path is hard. Yes, the barriers are real. But we need you—your vision, your grit, your commitment to positive impact, and your courage. The future of tech isn't just about the latest device or the coolest app. It's about who is sitting at the table when important decisions are made. It's about making sure that the tech we build is reflective of the diverse world we live in, that it serves *everyone*, and that it contributes to a more peaceful, harmonious society.

When you feel like giving up, remember why you started. Remember that the world needs more leaders like you—leaders who are ready to take risks, challenge the norms, and build a future that is more inclusive, more equitable, more peaceful, and more hopeful.

- **Purposeful Leadership**: Great leaders inspire not by their titles but by the values they live and the support they provide. What is the purpose driving your leadership, and how does it shape the way you uplift others?
- **Beyond Titles**: True influence isn't bound by your job title but by how you use your platform to lift others. How can you amplify voices in your field and create pathways for the next generation of leaders?
- **Impactful Choices**: True success is measured by the positive difference you make in others' lives. How can you ensure your daily decisions contribute to a legacy of empowerment and transformation?
- **Catalyst for Change**: Your expertise is a springboard for creating meaningful impact beyond your current role. Which nonprofit, private, or advisory boards align with your skills and passions?
- **Invest in Yourself**: Great leaders don't wait for opportunities—they prepare for them. How are you investing in your growth—whether through executive education, certifications, industry network memberships, or strategic events—to position yourself for board roles and high-impact leadership?
- **Investing in the Future**: Every decision you make is an investment—of time, energy, and resources. What choices can you make now to ensure your legacy drives positive change for years to come?

Conclusion: Break the Silicon Ceiling and Lead with Impact

When women rise, we all rise.

You didn't come this far to keep things as they are, did you? And I'm not just talking about reaching the end of this book—I'm talking about your journey in tech.

The **Chief in Tech Ambassador Program** is the next step, where you turn what you've learned into real, lasting change. This is your chance to lead.

It's time to take your experiences, wins, and even challenges, and use them to lift others. Whether it's mentoring, sharing your story, or starting conversations that matter, this program is for women ready to step up and lead the way forward.

Here's how you can make a difference:

- **Share Your Journey**: Claim your #ChiefInTech Ambassador badge and use the hashtag to share your story. Your voice can inspire others to break barriers and reach new heights.
- **Mentor and Empower**: Offer guidance to the next generation of women in tech leaders. From one-on-one mentorship to leading a circle, your insights can unlock doors and spark transformation.
- **Speak and Lead**: Run discussions, workshops, or speak at events that challenge the status quo and encourage others to take bold steps into leadership. Start locally, but think globally.

Ready to take the lead?

Join us at www.chiefintech.com/lead

Sign up today and connect with a global network of women pushing boundaries and leading the future of tech.

Let's build something bigger, together.

Notes

Chapter 1

1. WomenTech Network. Women in Tech Stats 2025. https://www.womentech.net/women-in-tech-stats

2. Global Gender Gap Report 2023. (n.d.). World Economic Forum. https://www.weforum.org/publications/global-gender-gap-report-2023/in-full/gender-gaps-in-the-workforce/

3. Siddhi Pal, Ruggero Marino Lazzaroni, and Paula Mendoza. "AI's Missing Link: The Gender Gap in the Talent Pool." Interface, October 10, 2024. https://www.interface-eu.org/publications/ai-gender-gap.

4. Carroll, S. (2024, September 26). Women in tech: A pathway to gender balance in top tech roles. *Grant Thornton International Ltd. Home.* https://www.grantthornton.global/en/insights/women-in-business/women-in-tech-a-pathway-to-gender-balance-in-top-tech-roles/

5. Accenture. "Resetting Tech Culture," accessed October 25, 2024. https://www.accenture.com/content/dam/accenture/final/a-com-migration/pdf/pdf-134/accenture-a4-gwc-report-final1.pdf#zoom=50

6. Veihmeyer, J., Doughtie, L., KPMG, & Ipsos. (n.d.). KPMG Women's Leadership Study. In *KPMG Women's Leadership Study.* https://assets.kpmg.com/content/dam/kpmg/ph/pdf/ThoughtLeadershipPublications/KPMGWomensLeadershipStudy.pdf

7. "The Impact of Stereotypes on Girls' Career Choices." n.d. Issuu. https://issuu.com/nyuappliedpsychology/docs/fall_2020_issue_v11/s/11823123

8. Veihmeyer, J., Doughtie, L., KPMG, & Ipsos. (n.d.). KPMG Women's Leadership Study. In *KPMG Women's Leadership Study*. https://assets .kpmg.com/content/dam/kpmg/ph/pdf/ThoughtLeadership Publications/KPMGWomensLeadershipStudy.pdf

9. Veihmeyer, J., Doughtie, L., KPMG, & Ipsos. (n.d.). KPMG Women's Leadership Study. In *KPMG Women's Leadership Study*. https://assets .kpmg.com/content/dam/kpmg/ph/pdf/ThoughtLeadership Publications/KPMGWomensLeadershipStudy.pdf

10. Radhika Krishnan, interview by author, August 7, 2024.

11. *Women in the Workplace 2022.* (2022b, October 18). McKinsey & Company. https://www.mckinsey.com/featured-insights/diversity-and-inclusion/women-in-the-workplace-archive#section-header-2022

12. *Women in the Workplace 2022.* (2022b, October 18). McKinsey & Company. https://www.mckinsey.com/featured-insights/diversity-and-inclusion/women-in-the-workplace-archive#section-header-2022

13. Matt Krentz, Justin Dean, Jennifer Garcia-Alonso, Frances Brooks Taplett, Miki Tsusaka, and Rainer Strack, "Dispelling the Myths of the Gender Ambition Gap," Boston Consulting Group, November 10, 2017, https:// www.bcg.com/publications/2017/people-organization-leadership-change-dispelling-the-myths-of-the-gender-ambition-gap

14. *Women leaders: does likeability really matter? | The Clayman Institute for Gender Research.* (2015, June 24). Stanford University. https://gender .stanford.edu/news/women-leaders-does-likeability-really-matter

15. Catalyst. 2007. *The Double-Bind Dilemma for Women in Leadership: Damned if You Do, Doomed if You Don't.* Catalyst. https://www.catalyst .org/wp-content/uploads/2019/01/The_Double_Bind_Dilemma_ for_Women_in_Leadership_Damned_if_You_Do_Doomed_if_ You_Dont.pdf

16. BBC News. (2017, December 13). *100 Women: "Why I invented the glass ceiling phrase."* https://www.bbc.com/news/world-42026266

17. Bruckmüller, S. (2017, September 7). *How Women End Up on the "Glass Cliff."* Harvard Business Review. https://hbr.org/2011/01/how-women-end-up-on-the-glass-cliff
Elliott, V. (2023, May 22). Twitter CEO Linda Yaccarino Is Teetering on the Glass Cliff. *WIRED.* https://www.wired.com/story/twitter-linda-yaccarino-glass-cliff/

18. "Glass cliffs: firms appoint female executives in times of crisis as a signal of change to investors." 2022. LSE Business Review. August 18, 2022. https://blogs.lse.ac.uk/businessreview/2022/08/19/glass-cliffs-firms-appoint-female-executives-in-times-of-crisis-as-a-signal-of-change-to-investors/

19. "Glass cliffs: firms appoint female executives in times of crisis as a signal of change to investors." 2022. LSE Business Review. August 18, 2022. https://blogs.lse.ac.uk/businessreview/2022/08/19/glass-cliffs-firms-appoint-female-executives-in-times-of-crisis-as-a-signal-of-change-to-investors/

20. Tremmel, M., & Wahl, I. (2023). Gender stereotypes in leadership: Analyzing the content and evaluation of stereotypes about typical, male, and female leaders. *Frontiers in Psychology, 14*. https://doi.org/10.3389/fpsyg.2023.1034258

21. Braun, S., Stegmann, S., Bark, A. S. H., Junker, N. M., & Van Dick, R. (2017). Think manager—think male, think follower—think female: Gender bias in implicit followership theories. *Journal of Applied Social Psychology, 47*(7), 377–388. https://doi.org/10.1111/jasp.12445

22. *The Language of Gender Bias in Performance Reviews.* (2022, September 6). Stanford Graduate School of Business. https://www.gsb.stanford.edu/insights/language-gender-bias-performance-reviews
    How to beat gender stereotypes: learn, speak up and react. (2024, September 10). World Economic Forum. https://www.weforum.org/agenda/2019/03/beat-gender-stereotypes-learn-speak-up-and-react/
    APA PsycNet. (n.d.). https://psycnet.apa.org/record/2015-56707-001

23. Player, A., De Moura, G. R., Leite, A. C., Abrams, D., & Tresh, F. (2019). Overlooked leadership potential: The preference for leadership potential in job candidates who are men vs. women. *Frontiers in Psychology, 10*. https://doi.org/10.3389/fpsyg.2019.00755
    Lyness, K. S., & Heilman, M. E. (2006). When fit is fundamental: Performance evaluations and promotions of upper-level female and male managers. *Journal of Applied Psychology, 91*(4), 777–785. https://doi.org/10.1037/0021-9010.91.4.777

24. Neveen Awad, interview by author, June 28, 2024.

25. Lori Nishiura Mackenzie, interview by author, June 27, 2024.

26. Elaine Montilla, interview by author, June 19, 2024.

27. Kramer, A. (2024, June 3). Why Women Face A Sound Barrier In Their Fight To Be Heard. *Forbes.* https://www.forbes.com/sites/andiekramer/2023/12/11/why-women-face-a-sound-barrier-in-their-fight-to-be-heard/
Carnegie Mellon University. (n.d.). *Women Interrupted: A New Strategy for Male-Dominated Discussions - News - Carnegie Mellon University.* https://www.cmu.edu/news/stories/archives/2020/october/women-interrupted-debate.html

28. Lang, C. (2020, October 9). 'Mr. Vice President, I'm Speaking.' What Research Says About Men Interrupting Women—And How to Stop It. *TIME.* https://time.com/5898144/men-interrupting-women/

29. KPMG International. (2022). Mind the Gap. In *KPMG International* (pp. 3–18). https://assets.kpmg.com/content/dam/kpmg/xx/pdf/2022/12/mind-the-gap.pdf

30. Kate Maxwell, interview by author, September 29, 2024.

31. Clance, P. R., Imes, S., Georgia State University, University Plaza, & Atlanta, Georgia 30303. (1978). The imposter phenomenon in high achieving women: dynamics and therapeutic intervention. In *Psychotherapy Theory, Research and Practice* (Vol. 15, Issue 3). https://www.paulineroseclance.com/pdf/ip_high_achieving_women.pdf

32. Penelope Prett, interview by author, August 9, 2024.

33. Clance, P. R., Imes, S., Georgia State University, University Plaza, & Atlanta, Georgia 30303. (1978). The imposter phenomenon in high achieving women: dynamics and therapeutic intervention. In *Psychotherapy Theory, Research and Practice* (Vol. 15, Issue 3). https://www.paulineroseclance.com/pdf/ip_high_achieving_women.pdf

34. Kathryn Guarini, interview by author, June 12, 2024.

35. Moskowitz, D. (2024, October 2). *The 10 Richest People in the World.* Investopedia. https://www.investopedia.com/articles/investing/012715/5-richest-people-world.asp

36. Reetal Pai, interview by author, June 18, 2024.

37. *2024 KPMG Women's Leadership Summit Report.* (n.d.). KPMG. https://kpmg.com/us/en/careers-and-culture/womens-leadership/summit/2024-kpmg-womens-leadership-summit-study.html

38. Daphne Jones, interview by author, Jun 27, 2024.

39. Sandberg, S. (2013). *Lean In: Women, Work, and the Will to Lead.* New York: Knopf.

Chapter 2

1. Dickerson, Craig. "The Ladder of Inference: Building Self-Awareness to Be A Better Human-Centered Leader." Harvard Business Publishing. May 9, 2024. https://www.harvardbusiness.org/the-ladder-of-inference-building-self-awareness-to-be-a-better-human-centered-leader/.

2. Ivneet Kaur, interview by author, June 12, 2024.

3. Holzel, B. K., Carmody, J., Vangel, M., Congleton, C., Yerramsetti, S. M., Gard, T., & Lazar, S. W. (2011). Mindfulness practice leads to increases in regional brain gray matter density. Psychiatry Research: Neuroimaging, 191(1), 36-43. https://pmc.ncbi.nlm.nih.gov/articles/PMC3004979/.

4. American Psychological Association. (2019). Mindfulness Meditation: A Research-Proven Way to Reduce Stress. Retrieved from https://www.apa.org/topics/mindfulness/meditation.

5. Aysha Khan, interview by author, July 11, 2024.

6. Brown, Brené. *Dare to Lead: Brave Work. Tough Conversations. Whole Hearts.* New York: Random House, 2018.

7. Kristof-brown, Amy L., Ryan D. Zimmerman, and Erin C. Johnson. 2005. "Consequences of individuals' fit at work: a meta-analysis of person–job, person–organization, person–group, and person–supervisor fit." *Personnel Psychology* 58 (2): 281–342. https://doi.org/10.1111/j.1744-6570.2005.00672.x.

8. Penelope Prett, interview by author, August 8, 2024.

9. Asha Keddy, interview by author, June 10, 2024.

10. "From careers to experiences: New pathways." n.d. Deloitte Insights. https://www2.deloitte.com/us/en/insights/focus/human-capital-trends/2018/building-21st-century-careers.html.

11. Deborah Corwin Scott, interview by author, July 2, 2024.

12. Zhuo, Julie. *The Making of a Manager: What to Do When Everyone Looks to You.* New York: Random House, 2019.

13. Keller, Scott. "Successfully transitioning to new leadership roles." McKinsey & Company. May 23, 2018. https://www.mckinsey.com/capabilities/people-and-organizational-performance/our-insights/successfully-transitioning-to-new-leadership-roles.

14. Keller, Scott. "Successfully transitioning to new leadership roles." McKinsey & Company. May 23, 2018. https://www.mckinsey.com/

capabilities/people-and-organizational-performance/our-insights/
successfully-transitioning-to-new-leadership-roles.

15. Fern Johnson, interview by author, July 2, 2024.

16. Kathryn Guarini, interview by author, June 12, 2024.

17. Linda Yao, Interview by author, June 17, 2024.

18. Watkins, Michael D. *The First 90 Days: Proven Strategies for Getting Up to Speed Faster and Smarter.* Updated and expanded ed. Boston: Harvard Business Review Press, 2013.

19. IBM Analytics. n.d. "The Employee Experience Index." https://info .enboarder.com/hubfs/PDF/The_Employee_Experience_Index.pdf.

20. Galante, Julieta, Claire Friedrich, Anna F Dawson, Marta Modrego-Alarcón, Pia Gebbing, Irene Delgado-Suárez, Radhika Gupta, et al. 2021. "Mindfulness-based programmes for mental health promotion in adults in nonclinical settings: A systematic review and meta-analysis of randomised controlled trials." *PLoS Medicine* 18 (1): e1003481. https://doi .org/10.1371/journal.pmed.1003481.

Bentley, Tanya G. K., Gina D'Andrea-Penna, Marina Rakic, Nick Arce, Michelle LaFaille, Rachel Berman, Katie Cooley, and Preston Sprimont. 2023. "Breathing practices for stress and anxiety reduction: conceptual framework of implementation guidelines based on a systematic review of the published literature." *Brain Sciences* 13 (12): 1612. https://doi .org/10.3390/brainsci13121612.

Chapter 3

1. Brand Builders Group. 2021. "Trends in Personal Branding - BBG - Brand Builders Group." November 3, 2021. https://brandbuildersgroup .com/study/.

2. Cohen, Ilene S. "Embrace Authenticity and Live Your True Self." *Psychology Today*, November 2023. https://www.psychologytoday.com/ intl/blog/your-emotional-meter/202311/embrace-authenticity-and-live-your-true-self.

3. Kathryn Guarini, interview by author, June 12, 2024.

4. Janet Robertson, interview by author, August 13, 2024.

5. Moss, Stan. "Creating a Culture of Trust: The How and Why Behind It." Inspiring Workplaces, November 15, 2023. https://www.

inspiring-workplaces.com/content/creating-a-culture-of-trust-the-how-and-why-behind-it/.

6. Goleman, Daniel. "Authentic Leadership and Emotional Intelligence." *Korn Ferry*, accessed November 7, 2024. https://www.kornferry.com/insights/this-week-in-leadership/authentic-leadership-emotional-intelligence.

7. Ibarra, Herminia. 2024. "The Authenticity Paradox." *Harvard Business Review*, May 3, 2024. https://hbr.org/2015/01/the-authenticity-paradox.

8. Rajalakshmi (Raji) Subramanian, interview by author, August 19, 2024.

9. Suman Rao, interview by author, August 2, 2024.

10. "Harnessing the Power of Stories | VMware Women's Leadership Innovation Lab." n.d. Stanford University. https://womensleadership .stanford.edu/node/796/harnessing-power-stories.

11. Tradenta, Julio Mancuso, Ananta Neelim, and Joe Vecci. "Self-Promotion, Social-Image and Gender Inequality: Aiding Women Break The Shackles of Modesty." *SSRN Electronic Journal*, January 2017. https://doi .org/10.2139/ssrn.3039233.

Chapter 4

1. Krawcheck, Sallie. "Your Network's Not Weak Enough." January 11, 2024. https://www.linkedin.com/pulse/your-networks-weak-enough-sallie-krawcheck-73lcc/.

2. Wolff, Hans-Georg, and Klaus Moser. 2009. "Effects of networking on career success: A longitudinal study." *Journal of Applied Psychology* 94 (1): 196–206. https://doi.org/10.1037/a0013350.

3. "The Network Effect: Why Companies Should Care About Employees' LinkedIn Connections." HBS Working Knowledge. November 14, 2023. https://hbswk.hbs.edu/item/the-network-effect-why-companies-should-care-about-employees-linkedin-connections.

4. Gabarro, John J., and John P. Kotter. "What Everyone Should Know About Managing Up." *Harvard Business Review*, January 2005. Accessed November 4, 2024. https://hbr.org/2015/01/what-everyone-should-know-about-managing-up

5. Devshree Golecha, interview by author, July 11, 2024.

6. LinkedIn Learning. 2023 Workplace Learning Report: Building the Agile Future. LinkedIn, 2023. Accessed November 4, 2024. https://learning.linkedin.com/resources/workplace-learning-report

7. "Manage stress: Strengthen your support network," October 22, 2024. https://www.apa.org/topics/stress/manage-social-support.

8. Edmondson, Amy C. "Wicked problem solvers: Lessons from successful cross-industry teams." *Harvard Business Review* 94, 6 (2016): 53–59. Accessed November 4, 2024. https://www.hbs.edu/faculty/Pages/item.aspx?num=51140

9. Grace Pérez, interview by author, June 24, 2024.

10. Stanford Graduate School of Business. "We Belong Together: How Communication Fuels Connection and Community." *Stanford Graduate School of Business*, 2021. Accessed November 4, 2024. https://www.gsb.stanford.edu/insights/we-belong-together-how-communication-fuels-connection-community

11. "CIPD | Effective cross-functional collaboration in a changing world of work." n.d. CIPD. https://www.cipd.org/uk/knowledge/reports/cross-functional-collaboration/.
"Organizational performance: It's a team sport." n.d. Deloitte Insights. https://www2.deloitte.com/us/en/insights/focus/human-capital-trends/2019/team-based-organization.html.

12. "Building Connective Communities with Margaux Miller." *Women in Tech Job Fair and Career Summit 2024*, YouTube. Accessed November 4, 2024. https://www.youtube.com/watch?v=TzSTr0H8GG8

13. LinkedIn. "About Us: Statistics." Accessed October 31, 2024. https://news.linkedin.com/about-us#Statistics.

14. Parna Sarkar-Basu, interview by author, July 9, 2024.

15. "Freeman Trends Report Q1 2024 - Freeman." October 18, 2024. https://www.freeman.com/resources/freeman-trends-report-q1-2024/.

16. Maximoff, Michael. "Sales follow-up statistics in B2B: Belkins' 2024 study." October 25, 2024. https://belkins.io/blog/sales-follow-up-statistics.

17. Walden University. 2022. "How Strategic Volunteering Can Positively Impact Your Career." *Walden University*, October 22, 2022. https://www.waldenu.edu/resource/how-strategic-volunteering-can-positively-impact-your-career.

18. "Ada Lovelace." *Britannica*. Accessed November 4, 2024. https://www.britannica.com/biography/Ada-Lovelace.

19. "Society of Women Engineers." *Wikipedia*, last modified October 30, 2023. https://en.wikipedia.org/wiki/Society_of_Women_Engineers

20. Milgram, Stanley. "The Small World Problem." *Psychology Today*, May 1967.

21. Novkova, Teodora. "Chief in Tech Executive Gala Dinner: Highlights, Takeaways, and Moments of Inspiration with Women in Tech Leaders." *WomenTech Network*, January 4, 2024. https://www.womentech.net/blog/chief-in-tech-executive-gala-dinner-highlights-takeaways-and-moments-inspiration-women-in-tech

22. Belli, Gina. "How Many Jobs Are Found Through Networking, Really?" Payscale - Salary Comparison, Salary Survey, Search Wages. September 19, 2023. https://www.payscale.com/career-advice/many-jobs-found-networking/.

Chapter 5

1. TED. "Great Mentors and Sponsors | Carla Harris." *TED Talks Daily* podcast. Transcript, accessed November 11, 2024. https://www.ted.com/podcasts/great-mentors-and-sponsors-carla-harris-transcript.

2. Gartner, Inc. Employee Mentoring Programs and Career Advancement: A Study of Promotion and Retention. Research study conducted for Sun Microsystems, 2006.

3. Siri Chilazi, interview by author, June 6, 2024.

4. Manju Abraham, interview by author, July 29, 2024.

5. Padmaja Dasari, interview by author, July 29, 2024.

6. Swetha Kolli, interview by author, June 25, 2024.

7. Suman Rao, interview by author, August 2, 2024.

8. Elaine Montilla, interview by author, June 19, 2024.

9. Linda Yao, interview by author, June 11, 2024.

10. Angelou, Maya. *Wouldn't Take Nothing for My Journey Now*. New York: Random House, 1993.

11. Sandy Carter, interview by author, June 13, 2024.

12. Grace Pérez, interview by author, June 24, 2024.

13. Janet Robertson, interview by author, August 13, 2024.

14. Cindy Taibi, interview by author, July 2, 2024.

15. Dana DiFerdinando, interview by author, August 1, 2024.

16. Rebecca Gasser, interview by author, June 26, 2024.

17. Dana DiFerdinando, interview by author, August 1, 2024.

18. Siri Chilazi, interview by author, June 6, 2024.

19. "The Sponsor Effect: Breaking Through the Last Glass Ceiling ^ 10428." n.d. HBR Store. https://store.hbr.org/product/the-sponsor-effect-breaking-through-the-last-glass-ceiling/10428?srsltid=AfmBOoozu1 TnTG3VdSWQr9e8szkB88RF8nqVdhm6NpjwVnic-8CFWkIu.

20. Siri Chilazi, interview by author, June 6, 2024.

21. Sylvia Ann Hewlett, *Forget a Mentor, Find a Sponsor* (Boston: Harvard Business Review Press, 2013).

22. Jennika Gold, interview by author, June 13, 2024.

23. Asha Keddy, interview by author, June 10, 2024.

24. Manju Abraham, interview by author, July 29, 2024.

25. Deepna Devkar, interview by August 13, 2024.

26. Anuradha Dodda, interview by author, July 12, 2024.

27. Fern Johnson, interview by author, July 2, 2024.

28. Grace Pérez, interview by author, June 24, 2024.

29. Korn Ferry. *Real World Leadership Study: Lack of Executive Sponsorship as a Key Barrier to Leadership Development.* December 10, 2015. Accessed November 1, 2024. https://www.kornferry.com/about-us/press/korn-ferry-global-study-cites-lack-of-executive-sponsorship-as-the-chief-roadblock-to-leadership-development-success.

30. Siri Chilazi, interview by author, June 6, 2024.

31. DuBow, Wendy M., and Catherine Ashcraft. "Exploring the role of male allies in gender diversity within the technology sector." *International Journal of Gender, Science and Technology* 11, 2 (2019): 297–314. Accessed November 11, 2024. https://genderandset.open.ac.uk/index.php/genderandset/article/download/379/780.

32. Empovia. Allyship Report, April 2023. https://empovia.co/wp-content/uploads/2023/04/Allyship-Report-Empovia.pdf.

33. Monique J. Morrow, interview by author, June 12, 2024.

34. Nadine Thomson, interview by author, July 5, 2024.

35. Elaine Montilla, interview by author, June 19, 2024.

36. Swetha Kolli, interview by author, June 25, 2024.

37. Harvard Business Publishing Corporate Learning. *2021 Pulse Report: Organizational Diversity, Inclusion, and Belonging.* Accessed October 31, 2024. https://www.harvardbusiness.org/insight/2021-pulse-report-organizational-diversity-inclusion-and-belonging/.

38. Adams, Titina Ott. "Building Your Own Board of Directors – The Importance of Networking." Women in Tech Global Conference, YouTube video, [18:24], posted 21 December 2021. https://www.youtube.com/watch?v=LGjVb8O2l3I.

39. Gibson, D'Lovely. "Building a Board of Directors to Ensure Your Growth and Development." *Women in Tech Global Awards,* Accessed November 11, 2024. https://dev.womentech.net/video/building-board-directors-ensure-your-growth-and-development-dlovely-gibson

40. Sandy Carter, interview by author, June 13, 2024.

41. Allen, Tammy D., Lillian T. Eby, Mark L. Poteet, Elizabeth Lentz, and Lizzette Lima. 2004. "Career benefits associated with mentoring for proteges: A meta-analysis." *Journal of Applied Psychology* 89 (1): 127–36. https://doi.org/10.1037/0021-9010.89.1.127.

42. "Case Study: Workforce Analytics at Sun." 2006. *Gartner.* https://www.gartner.com/en/documents/497507.

43. *BDC.Ca.* "How an advisory board can boost your business." August 1, 2024. https://www.bdc.ca/en/articles-tools/business-strategy-planning/manage-business/can-advisory-board-help-grow.

44. Change Catalyst. *The State of Allyship Report: The Key to Workplace Inclusion.* San Francisco, CA: Change Catalyst, 2021. Accessed November 12, 2024. https://ccwestt-ccfsimt.org/wp-content/uploads/2023/07/TheStateofAllyshipReport-by-ChangeCatalyst-v1-1.pdf.

Chapter 6

1. Gates, Melinda. *The Moment of Lift: How Empowering Women Changes the World.* New York: Flatiron Books, 2019.

2. Bhawna Singh, interview by author, June 10, 2024.

3. Reetal Pai, interview by author, June 18, 2024.

4. Linda Yao, interview by author, June 11, 2024.

5. Vivienne Wei, interview by author, August 12, 2024.

6. Fern Johnson, interview by author, July 2, 2024.

7. Nirmal Srinivasan, interview by author, August 11, 2024.

8. Nadine Thomson, interview by author, July 5, 2024.

9. Lori Nishiura Mackenzie, interview by author, June 27, 2024.

10. Carol S. Dweck, *Mindset: The New Psychology of Success* (New York: Random House, 2006).

11. Ospina, Sonia M., and Erica Gabrielle Foldy. "Collaborative leadership and the circular nature of power: building innovation in teams." *Journal of Public Administration Research and Theory* 30, 3 (2020): 495–511. https://www.tandfonline.com/doi/pdf/10.1080/14719037.2020.1743344.

12. Radulovski, Anna. "Hispanic Heritage Month: An Exclusive Conversation with Maria B. Winans, CMO of Kyndryl, on Leadership, Innovation, and Inclusion in Tech." Women in Tech Network. September 16, 2024. https://www.womentech.net/blog/hispanic-heritage-month-exclusive-conversation-maria-b-winans-cmo-kyndryl-leadership.

13. Rebecca Gasser, interview by author, June 26, 2024.

14. Truist Leadership Institute. Executive Presence: Disrupting What We Think We Know. Accessed November 16, 2024. https://www.truistleadershipinstitute.com/content/dam/truistleadershipinstitute/us/en/documents/executive-presence.pdf.

15. Center for Talent Innovation. Executive Presence: The Missing Link Between Merit and Success. Coqual. Accessed November 16, 2024. https://coqual.org/wp-content/uploads/2020/09/26_executivepresence_keyfindings-1.pdf.

16. Parna Sarkar-Basu, interview by author, July 9, 2024.

17. Bass, Bernard M., and Ronald E. Riggio. 2006. *Transformational Leadership*. 2nd ed. Mahwah, NJ: Lawrence Erlbaum Associates.

18. Tactyqal. "From Rejections to Billions: The Melanie Perkins Success Story." Tactyqal. Accessed November 1, 2024. https://www.tactyqal.com/blog/melanie-perkins-success-story-rejections-to-billions/.

19. Forbes Australia (2024) *Canva steamrolls on as valuation climbs $10bn to $49bn*. Available at: https://www.forbes.com.au/news/entrepreneurs/canva-steamrolls-on-as-valuation-climbs-10bn-to-49bn/

20. Manju Abraham, interview by author, July 29, 2024.

21. Suman Rao, interview by author, August 2, 2024.

22. Sousa, Michel, and Dirk Van Dierendonck. "Introducing a short measure of shared servant leadership impacting team performance through team behavioral integration." *Frontiers in Psychology* 6 (2015): 2002. https://www.frontiersin.org/journals/psychology/articles/10.3389/fpsyg.2015.02002/full.

23. Sundar Pichai's Leadership Style: Running Google." Pressfarm. Accessed November 16, 2024. https://press.farm/sundar-pichais-leadership-style-running-google/.

24. Deloitte. "Six Signature Traits of Inclusive Leadership." Deloitte Insights. Last modified January 14, 2016. https://www2.deloitte.com/us/en/insights/topics/talent/six-signature-traits-of-inclusive-leadership.html.

25. Anne Carrigy, interview by author, August 9, 2024.

26. Linda Yao, interview by author, June 11, 2024.

27. Duarte, Ana Patrícia, Neuza Ribeiro, Ana Suzete Semedo, and Daniel Roque Gomes. 2021. "Authentic leadership and improved individual performance: affective commitment and individual creativity's sequential mediation." *Frontiers in Psychology* 12 (May). https://doi.org/10.3389/fpsyg.2021.675749.

28. Dean, Katherine W. n.d. "Values-Based Leadership: How Our Personal Values Impact the Workplace." *The Journal of Values-Based Leadership*, Vol. 1, Issue 1. ValpoScholar. https://scholar.valpo.edu/jvbl/vol1/iss1/9/.

29. Monique J. Morrow, interview by author, June 12, 2024.

30. Reeny Sondhi, interview by author, August 28, 2024.

31. Reetal Pai, interview by author, June 18, 2024.

32. Deborah Corwin Scott, interview by author, July 2, 2024.

33. Rebecca Parsons, interview by author, August 5, 2024.

34. Glassdoor. "Four in Five (81%) Employees Say They're Motivated to Work Harder When Their Boss Shows Appreciation for Their Work, According to Glassdoor Survey." Last modified September 18, 2013. https://www.glassdoor.com/about/press-release/employees-stay-longer-company-bosses-showed-appreciation-glassdoor-survey/.

35. Devshree Golecha, interview by author, July 11, 2024.

36. Von Bergen, C. W., Jr., Martin S. Bressler, Kitty Campbell, and Southeastern Oklahoma State University. 2014. The sandwich feedback method: Not very tasty. *Journal of Behavioral Studies in Business*. Vol. 7. https://aabri.com/manuscripts/141831.pdf.

37. Scott, Kim. 2017. *Radical Candor: How to Get What You Want by Saying What You Mean*. Pan Macmillan.

38. Gallup. State of the American Workplace. Washington, D.C.: Gallup, 2017. https://www.gallup.com/workplace/238085/state-american-workplace-report-2017.aspx.

39. Glassdoor. "Employers Could Retain Half of Their Employees Longer if Bosses Showed More Appreciation, Glassdoor Survey Finds." Last modified September 18, 2013. https://www.glassdoor.com/blog/employers-to-retain-half-of-their-employees-longer-if-bosses-showed-more-appreciation-glassdoor-survey/.

Chapter 7

1. Beshay. "When Negotiating Starting Salaries, Most U.S. Women and Men Don't Ask for Higher Pay." *Pew Research Center*, April 14, 2024. https://www.pewresearch.org/short-reads/2023/04/05/when-negotiating-starting-salaries-most-us-women-and-men-dont-ask-for-higher-pay/.
2. Mazei, Jens, Joachim Hüffmeier, Philipp Alexander Freund, Alice F. Stuhlmacher, Lena Bilke, and Guido Hertel. 2015. "A meta-analysis on gender differences in negotiation outcomes and their moderators." *Psychological Bulletin* 141 (1): 85–104
3. Institute for Women's Policy Research. *Annual Gender Wage Gap by Race and Ethnicity* (2022).
4. Mazei, Jens, Joachim Hüffmeier, Philipp Alexander Freund, Alice F. Stuhlmacher, Lena Bilke, and Guido Hertel. 2015. "A meta-analysis on gender differences in negotiation outcomes and their moderators." *Psychological Bulletin* 141 (1): 85–104
5. Nadine Thomson, interview by author, July 5, 2024.
6. Staff, CyberWire. "The FBI Hostage Negotiator - with Chris Voss." *N2K CyberWire*, October 16, 2024. https://thecyberwire.com/podcasts/spycast/655/transcript.
7. Wendy Gonzalez, interview by author, August 12, 2024.
8. Penelope Prett, interview by author, August 9, 2024.
9. Deepna Devkar, interview by August 13, 2024.
10. Rebecca Gasser, interview by author, June 26, 2024.
11. Jennika Gold, interview by author, June 13, 2024.
12. Grace Pérez, interview by author, June 24, 2024.
13. Deborah Corwin Scott, interview by author, July 2, 2024.
14. Dana DiFerdinando, interview by author, August 1, 2024.
15. Reetal Pai, interview by author, June 18, 2024.
16. Janet Robertson, interview by author, August 13, 2024.
17. Vivienne Wei, interview by author, August 12, 2024.
18. AESC and BlueSteps. 2016. "2016 BlueSteps Job Outlook." Report. *AESC.Org - BlueSteps.Com.* https://www.aesc.org/sites/default/files/uploads/documents-2015/2016-AESC-BlueSteps-Executive-Job-Outlook.pdf.

19. University of Pittsburgh. "'The No Club' empowers women to take control of their professional lives." May 2, 2022. https://www.pitt.edu/pittwire/features-articles/no-club-empowers-women-lise-vesterlund.

Chapter 8

1. Hayes, Mary, Frances Chumney, Marcus Buckingham, and Workplace. 2020. "Workplace Resilience Study Full Research Report." *Workplace Resilience Study Full Research Report.* https://www.adpresearch.com/wp-content/uploads/2020/09/R0120_0920_v1FINAL_RS_ResearchReport_040621.pdf.

2. Duckworth, Angela. 2016. *Grit: The Power of Passion and Perseverance.* Random House.

3. "Serena Williams: A Trailblazing Odyssey of Empowerment, Equality, and Global Impact." Amazons Watch Magazine. Accessed October 29, 2024. https://www.amazonswatchmagazine.com/others/impact-inspire/serena-williams-a-trailblazing-odyssey-of-empowerment-equality-and-global-impact/.

4. Maria B. Winans, interview by author, September 10, 2024.

5. Maria B. Winans, interview by author, September 10, 2024.

6. Ivneet Kaur, interview by author, June 18, 2024.

7. Ivneet Kaur, interview by author, June 18, 2024.

8. Nirmal Srinivasan, interview by author, August 11, 2024.

9. Bharadwaj, Anu. "Long-term Resilience: How to Manage Your Energy to Manage Your Time." YouTube. Accessed October 29, 2024. https://www.youtube.com/watch?v=Tsf8qbW8q1M.

10. Denise Lee Yeh, interview by author, August 2, 2024.

11. Elaine Zhou, interview by author, July 9, 2024.

12. Manju Abraham, interview by author, July 29, 2024.

13. Thangavelu, Poonkulali. "Companies that Failed to Innovate and Went Bankrupt." Investopedia, September 30, 2024. https://www.investopedia.com/articles/investing/072115/companies-went-bankrupt-innovation-lag.asp.

14. Asana Team. "The Eisenhower Matrix: How to Prioritize Your To-Do List [2024] • Asana." *Asana,* January 29, 2024. https://asana.com/resources/eisenhower-matrix.

15. Women in Tech Network. *Women in Tech Global Conference 2024: Keynote by Archana Jain*. Accessed October 29, 2024. https://www.youtube.com/watch?v=J9FbF56pZgs

16. "A quote by A.P.J. Abdul Kalam." n.d. https://www.goodreads.com/quotes/1015959---if-you-fail-never-give-up-because-f-a-i-l-means.

17. "Girls Who Code Founder Reshma Saujani on Fighting for Mothers Rights And Taking Risks." n.d. https://www.thewiesuite.com/post/girls-who-code-founder-reshma-saujani-on-fighting-for-mothers-rights-tech-s-retention-problem.

18. Denise Lee Yeh, interview by author, August 2, 2024.

19. Hayes Mary, Frances Chumney, Marcus Buckingham, and ADP Research Institute. 2020. "10 Facts About Resilience." *Workplace Resilience Study Executive Summary*. ADP, Inc. https://www.adpresearch.com/wp-content/uploads/2020/09/R0121_0920_v1_RS_ExecSummary.pdf.

Chapter 9

1. Brown, Brené. *Daring Greatly: How the Courage to Be Vulnerable Transforms the Way We Live, Love, Parent, and Lead*. New York: Gotham Books, 2012. Goodreads. Accessed November 19, 2024. https://www.goodreads.com/quotes/7187011-we-don-t-have-to-do-all-of-it-alone-we

2. Stephanie Domas, interview by author, July 5, 2024.

3. Ernst & Young. "How Gen Z Is Redefining Success for Decades to Come." EY.com, accessed January 13, 2025. https://www.ey.com/en_us/insights/consulting/how-gen-z-is-redefining-success-for-decades-to-come

4. Wikipedia. 2024. "Time Management." Last modified January 19, 2024. https://en.wikipedia.org/wiki/Time_management

5. Reeny Sondhi, interview by author, August 28, 2024.

6. Janet Robertson, interview by author, August 13, 2024.

7. Stephanie Domas, interview by author, July 5, 2024.

8. *The Free-Time Gender Gap*. Gender Equity Policy Institute, 2022. https://thegepi.org/the-free-time-gender-gap/

9. Women in the Workplace 2024. (2024). In leanin.org. LeanIn.Org and McKinsey & Company. https://cdn-static.leanin.org/women-in-the-workplace/2024-pdf

10. McKinsey & Company and LeanIn.Org. *Women in the Workplace 2024: The 10th Anniversary Report*. McKinsey & Company, 2024. https://www.mckinsey.com/featured-insights/themes/women-in-the-workplace-parity-for-all-women-is-almost-50-years-away

11. Ella Scott. "Woman Hits Back After Being Slammed for Crying Over 9 to 5 Job." *Tyla*, October 27, 2023. https://www.tyla.com/life/true-life/9-to-5-job-crying-tiktok-brielle-asero-888173-20231027

12. Padmaja Dasari, interview by author, July 29, 2024.

13. *The State of Meetings in 2019: Insights and Trends*. (n.d.). Doodle. https://doodle.com/en/resources/research-and-reports-/the-state-of-meetings-2019/

14. Aysha Khan, interview by author, July 11, 2024.

15. Sandy Carter, interview by author, June 13, 2024.

16. Sheryl Sandberg, *Lean In: Women, Work, and the Will to Lead* (New York: Knopf, 2013). https://www.penguinrandomhouse.com/books/220839/lean-in-by-sheryl-sandberg/

Chapter 10

1. Aaron Pressman. "AMD CEO Has Advice for MIT Grads." *Fortune*, June 9, 2021. https://fortune.com/2017/06/09/dont-want-to-work-for-no-harvard-mbas/

2. Asha Keddy, interview by author, June 10, 2024.

3. Atkins, Betsy. *Be Board Ready: The Secrets to Landing a Board Seat and Being a Great Director*. New York: BookBaby, 2019.

4. Daphne E. Jones, interview by author, Jun 27, 2024.

5. PitchBook Data, Inc. *All In: Women in the VC Ecosystem*. Seattle: Pitch-Book, 2020.

6. Monique J. Morrow, interview by author, June 12, 2024.

7. "5 Female-Founded Venture Capital Funds to Know — and the Startups They Support." *Business Insider*. Accessed October 30, 2024. https://www.businessinsider.com/guides/female-founded-venture-capital-funds-startups-investments

8. Global Impact Investing Network. "Achieving the Sustainable Development Goals: The Role of Impact Investing." *The GIIN*, September 8, 2017. https://thegiin.org/publication/research/sdgs-impinv

9. "Empathic Leaders Drive Employee Engagement and Innovation." *Catalyst*, September 14, 2021. https://www.catalyst.org/media-release/empathic-leaders-drive-employee-engagement-and-innovation-media-release/

Acknowledgments

This book would not exist without the brilliant minds and generous hearts of so many people who've taught me, supported me, and challenged me to think bigger. To the WomenTech Network community—your passion, energy, and commitment to our mission have been a constant reminder of why this work matters. Together, we've built something extraordinary—a global network of 150,000+ members creating real, measurable impact.

To my husband, Ivo, and my daughter, Sophia—your love, encouragement, and belief in me have been my greatest source of strength. To my mother, whose support has been my foundation—thank you for always cheering me on.

To the remarkable leaders whose journeys are captured in these pages: Anne Carrigy, Anu Bharadwaj, Anuradha Dodda, Asha Keddy, Archana Jain, Aysha Khan, Bhawna Singh, Cindy Taibi, Dana DiFerdinando, Daphne E. Jones, Deborah Corwin Scott, Deepna Devkar, Denise Lee Yeh, Devshree Golecha, D'Lovely Gibson, Elaine Montilla, Elaine Zhou, Fern Johnson, Grace Pérez, Ivneet Kaur, Janet Robertson, Jennie Baird, Jennika Gold, Kate Maxwell, Kathryn Guarini, Linda Yao, Lori Nishiura Mackenzie, Louise Buson, Manju Abraham, Maria B. Winans, Monique Jeanne Morrow, Nadine Thomson, Neveen Awad, Nirmal Srinivasan, Padmaja Dasari, Parna Sarkar-Basu, Penelope Prett, Rachel Potvin, Radhika Krishnan, Raji Subramanian, Rebecca Gasser, Rebecca Parsons, Reeny Sondhi, Reetal Pai, Sandy Carter, Siri Chilazi, Stephanie Domas, Suman Rao, Swetha Kolli, Titina Ott Adams, Vijaya Kaza, Vivienne Wei, and Wendy Gonzalez, Wendy M. Pfeiffer—thank you for generously sharing your stories, your wisdom, and for proving what's possible when women lead with intention and courage.

To the whole WomenTech Network team—especially Angelina, Jasmin, Lori, and Maybel—thank you for your support, insights, and thoughtful feedback.

To Wiley Publishing, especially Christina Verigan, Deborah Williams, and Victoria Savanh—your professionalism, expertise, and patience have been invaluable. Thank you for guiding this book to life with such care and precision.

To the readers of *Chief in Tech*—thank you for investing your time and energy in these pages. This book is a conversation, a blueprint for impact, and a spark for innovation. My hope is that it leaves you empowered to lead boldly and to lift others as you rise.

And to the trailblazers who've inspired us all—visionaries like Ginni Rometty, Mira Murati, and Sheryl Sandberg—your leadership, innovation, and resilience reminds us that progress is driven by those brave enough to lead.

Together, we are breaking barriers, making an impact or making a difference, and building a future where women in tech thrive as leaders of change.

With infinite gratitude,
Anna Radulovski

Index

boundaries
  and flexibility, 158
  non-negotiable, 163
  professional, 140
  pushing, 10, 14, 76, 104, 136
  setting, 66, 78, 133, 156–7
Brand and Buzz Consulting,
    57, 97
Brand Builders Group, 30
brand consistency, 34
bro culture, 5
broken rung concept, 3
Brown, Brené, 19, 149
Bumble, 93

C
Calm app, 17
Canva, 98–9
career identity, 16–18
Carnegie Mellon University, 118
Carrigy, Anne, 100, 123–4
Carter, Sandy, 77, 88, 161–2
Challengers, 73–76
ChatGPT, 39, 77, 143, 154
Chilazi, Siri, 73, 76, 80, 84, 119
Choreograph, 86, 95, 119
Cisco, 80, 140
clarity
  for accountability, 107–8, 110
  and conflict, 107
  in effective communication, 94
  energy for, 162
  and fulfillment, 20
  in impact-driven ventures, 176
  from mentors, 78
  and mindfulness, 18

"no" as a tool for, 159
  and self-awareness, 27
  from sponsors, 82
  from Strategists, 74
  in teams, 105
  visualization for, 25
Code.org, 171
Coding Girls, 87–8
collaboration
  advice as, 63
  in authentic leadership, 101–2
  and communication, 95
  cross-departmental, 21
  in cross-functional projects, 19,
    25, 55–6, 116
  cross-industry, 55
  delegation for, 154
  and empathy, 94, 98
  as events, 59–60
  fostering, 22, 25
  in holistic leadership, 103
  between humans and
    machines, 143
  in hybrid work, 159
  importance of, 37–8, 129
  and inclusivity, 96
  leadership for, 37, 92, 96,
    100–1, 108, 147
  and legacies, 180
  on LinkedIn, 57–8
  and mentorship, 23
  mindset of, 121
  networking as, 64, 66
  online, 56
  and promotions, 123
  and psychological safety, 111